GOD IN

Owned by:

_____

Given by:

_____

Date: _____

Message:

Happy anniversary, Arizona!

Since its publication in 2007, "God in the Foundations of Arizona Government" has informed many local, state and federal elected officials, a wide cross-section of the Christian community, including pastors and intercessors, as well as those who simply care about Arizona history.

This book fuels a deeper understanding of God's heart for Arizona—our place in history—and makes the centennial celebration even more meaningful. It is helping to re-awaken the knowledge of God's invited presence in the government and foundations of our state. It is also serving to actually add to the official record of God in Arizona government!

In the last three years, I have submitted four requests for state proclamations for prayer which have been issued by Arizona governors. Chapter 4 on the "Treaties to Secure the Land of Arizona" inspired the formation of the Mexico-USA Border Prayer Alliance in 2008, which I serve as U.S. coordinator. Many of the powerful prayers of Chaplain Seaborn Crutchfield, recorded in Chapter 7, are now sometimes used to open up legislative sessions and at countless prayer events. Thousands of Arizona citizens are learning that Arizona's official state motto in Latin, *Ditat Deus*, means "God Enriches."

I hope you enjoy and benefit from this research no matter your reason for reading it. May God bless and enrich you!

- Guy Chadwick, May 2011

GOD
IN THE
FOUNDATIONS
OF
ARIZONA
GOVERNMENT

W. GUY CHADWICK

Published by
Arizona Call to Prayer
Phoenix, Arizona

First Edition, Third Printing: May 2011

COVER IMAGES AND PHOTOGRAPHS:

Upper Center (in the "O" of "GOD")... for this special centennial printing we have replaced the original Territorial Seal of Arizona of earlier printings with the new official Arizona Centennial emblem.

Upper row, far left... President Abraham Lincoln, 1861 portrait, public domain.

Upper row, 2nd from left... John N. Goodwin, first Arizona Territorial Governor, who led the governmental party of 1863 and convened the first Arizona Territorial legislative session in Prescott in 1864, *by permission of the Arizona Historical Foundation.*

Upper row, 3rd from left... the original proclamation of the U.S. Territory of Arizona, signed on December 29, 1863 at Navajo Springs, Arizona, organizing the first territorial government, *courtesy of the Arizona State Library, Archives and Public Records.*

Upper row, far right... Richard C. McCormick, first Arizona Territorial Secretary and second territorial Governor, who brought the Arizona Territorial Seal and Motto with him in 1863, *public domain from Wikipedia, the free on-line encyclopedia.*

Lower row, far left... Territorial Governor Louis C. Hughes, c.1890, by permission of Arizona State Library, Archives and Public Records, #99-9643

Lower row, 2nd from left... 1894 Arizona Territorial Thanksgiving Day Proclamation, courtesy of Arizona State Library, Archives and Public Records

Lower row, 3rd from left... Marcus Aurelius Smith, one of the first two U.S. Senators from Arizona; served multiple terms as Arizona territorial delegate, and was key in the congressional battle to preserve Arizona as an independent state from being absorbed into New Mexico, *public domain courtesy of the Biographical Directory of the U.S. Congress.*

Lower row, far right... Reverend Seaborn Crutchfield, at age 88 in 1925, who at age 73, served as chaplain for the Arizona Constitutional Convention of 1910, and remained active as legislative chaplain until the year of his death at age 90 in 1927, *by permission of the Arizona State Library, Archives and Public Records,* #99-9626

Additional photograph and image credits are given in the Appendix on page 177.

Cover design and overall layout by Guy Chadwick

WRITTEN & COMPILED BY W. GUY CHADWICK

Unless otherwise noted, scripture taken from *The Holy Bible*, New King James Version, Copyright © 1982 by Thomas Nelson, Inc.

Published by *Arizona Call to Prayer*
A ministry of *BridgeBuilders Int'l Leadership Network*
P.O. Box 31415, Phoenix, AZ 85046-1415 / 602-977-1111
E-Mail: info@arizonacalltoprayer.org / Website: www.arizonacalltoprayer.net

Printed by *D&L Press* - Phoenix, Arizona

ISBN #978-0-9795707-0-4

First Edition, Third Printing: May 2011

All rights reserved.

*"If the foundations are destroyed,
what can the righteous do?"*
- Psalm 11:3

A PRAYER FOR GOOD GOVERNMENT

"Lord, today I appeal to a higher court than the court of this land and I present my plea before an authority greater than any found on earth. Lord, I stand before the court of heaven and cry out for justice from the one, true, Judge of the earth. God, I cry out to You for righteous leaders in the government of America. Lord, day after day I will present my earnest petition before you... Give America men and women who stand righteous before you that they may be able to discern true justice. Restore to the government of this nation, men and women as of old. Raise up equals to our Founding Fathers, who knew their God and the severity of the covenant in which their country walked. Amen."

–Tiffani Edwards, age 23, April 3, 2007
Justice House of Prayer, Washington, DC

For

Arizona's Government Leaders

"He has told you, O man, what is good; and what does the Lord require of you but to do justly, to love mercy, and to walk humbly with your God?"
– Micah 6:8

And all those who pray for them

*"Therefore I exhort first of all
that supplications, prayers, intercessions,
and giving of thanks be made for all men,
for kings and all who are in authority,
that we may lead a quiet and peaceable life
in all godliness and reverence.
For this is good and acceptable in the sight
of God our Savior, who desires all men to be saved
and to come to the knowledge of the truth."*
– 1 Timothy 2:1-4

TABLE of CONTENTS

	A Prayer for Good Government 4
	Foreword I by Len Munsil, Esq. 8
	Foreword II by Cheryl Sacks 12
	Population Growth History 13
	Preface 14
I.	Introduction 16
	A Simple Timeline of Our History 23
II.	Biblical Foundations 24
III.	Our National Foundations 28
IV.	The Treaties to Secure the Land of Arizona 40
V.	The New Arizona Territory – 1863 44
VI.	The Arizona Constitutional Convention of 1910 and Biography of Chaplain Seaborn Crutchfield 70
VII.	The Prayers of Chaplain Seaborn Crutchfield 80
	Table of Contents for Crutchfield's Prayers 82
	A Note to Intercessors 83
VIII.	Preamble to the Arizona Constitution 138
IX.	Arizona State Seal and Motto 144
X.	Arizona Statehood Day - February 14, 1912 152
	The Genesis of Government 155
XI.	Conclusion 156
	A Few Verses Regarding Prayer 159

Appendix
  i. Solemn Assembly, State Capitol – 2002 160
  ii. Recent Arizona prayer journey accounts 161
  iii. Resources and References 174
  iv. Photography and Image Credits 177
  v. About the Author .... Inside Back Cover

DEDICATION & THANKS

I wish to dedicate this book to my gorgeous wife, Teri; our great kids, Kia, Dane, and Garin; and my parents, George and Rosalie—for their unfailing life-long support.

I especially would like to recognize my best friends and 'mountaintop' buddies, Len Munsil and Louie McGeorge. Special thanks to Len and Cheryl Sacks for writing Forewords to this book and for helping to bring me into a leadership role of governmental prayer for Arizona.

Deep appreciation to many good friends in this adventure, including Daniel and Gwen Brymer and family, Len and Tracy Munsil and family, Hal and Cheryl Sacks, Kathleen Graham, Curt and Rhonda Edwards and family, Hector and Janelle Ortiz, David and Helen Hook and family, Joyce LaMance, Jewel Gates, Deb Fritch, Bruce and Anita Hensley, Arizona Legislative Chaplain Jon McHatton, Arizona Senate President Tim Bee, Arizona Representative Nancy Barto, and all those who are a part of the staff and support of *Arizona Call to Prayer* and my former associates at *The Center for Arizona Policy*, and so many others stationed in prayer throughout Arizona.

I extend a special thank you to Archivists Wendi Goen and Nancy Sawyer who have gone the extra mile for me at the *Arizona State Library, Archives and Public Records* department at the State Capitol. In fact, every staff person at the libraries and archives I have frequented has been very gracious.

Above all, this is dedicated to my Savior and Lord, Jesus Christ.

> *"My heart is overflowing with a good theme;*
> *I recite my composition concerning the King;*
> *My tongue is the pen of a ready writer."*
> *– Psalm 45:1*

FOREWORD I *by Len Munsil, Esq.*

It was a long, hot summer. And the delegates to the Constitutional Convention in Philadelphia were cranky. They had been unable to agree on much of anything, let alone fundamental issues like how the individual states were to be represented in the new national Congress.

It fell to one man to turn America's leaders back to God. And he was an unlikely choice in a convention filled with Christian clergy and other devout Christian leaders – an open Deist who contributed to all Christian denominations but claimed fidelity to none.

On June 28, 1787, Benjamin Franklin, then 81 years of age and as Governor of Pennsylvania, host of the gathering in his home state, rose to speak:

"Mr. President, the small progress we have made after four or five weeks...is methinks a melancholy proof of the imperfection of the Human Understanding....

"In this situation of this Assembly, groping as it were in the dark to find political truth...how has it happened, sir, that we have not hitherto once thought of humbly applying to the Father of Lights to illuminate our understanding?

"In the beginning of the contest with Great Britain, when we were sensible of danger, we had daily prayer in the room for Divine Protection. Our prayers, sir, were heard, and they were graciously answered....

"And have we now forgotten that powerful Friend? Or do we imagine we no longer need His assistance?

*"I have lived, sir, a long time, and the longer I live the more convincing proofs I see of this truth – **that God governs in the affairs of men. And if a sparrow cannot***

fall to the ground without his notice, is it probable that an empire can rise without His aid?

"We have been assured, sir, in the Sacred Writings, that 'except the Lord build the house, they labor in vain who build it.' I firmly believe this; and I also believe that without His concurring aid we shall succeed in this political building no better than the builders of Babel..."

On Franklin's urging, the Constitutional Convention quickly passed a resolution to begin each session in prayer. (Ironically, that prayer resolution was offered by James Madison – the author of the very same First Amendment that is today used to ban prayer at governmental proceedings.)

And again, the prayers of the delegates were answered. As one delegate reported, when the convention "assembled again" and began with prayer, "... every unfriendly feeling had been expelled, and a spirit of conciliation had been cultivated."

About 123 years later the founding fathers of Arizona gathered in Phoenix to begin the process of creating an Arizona Constitution.

In Phoenix, although it was unquestionably hotter than Philadelphia (but a dry heat!), there was no dramatic moment when the contentious delegates realized they needed to hit their knees in prayer.

Instead, it appears Ben Franklin's view of the need for prayer was universally recognized from the beginning of the Arizona Convention. The framers of Arizona's Constitution seemed to recognize that if a sparrow could not "fall to the ground without His notice," no new state would "rise without His aid."

How else explain a constitutional convention whose every day was bathed in specific, detailed and compelling prayer?

Perhaps because of this foundational prayer covering, Arizona was spared the contentious deliberations, crises and impasses that plagued the Philadelphia convention.

Rev. Seaborn Crutchfield's prayers were not only reported in the daily press at the time, but they were recorded right alongside the deliberations of the delegates in permanent, official journals of the convention.

And it should be no surprise that thankfulness to "Almighty God" from the people of Arizona was enshrined in the actual text of the Arizona Constitution's preamble.

As a constitutional lawyer, I am astounded by those who want to expunge from the history books the profound Christian faith and prayer of those who founded our nation and our state.

Religious freedom is not threatened by a simple recognition of our Christian heritage. And non-partisan prayer for elected officials and for good government does not threaten to impose religion on anyone.

We need to recognize, as Franklin did, that the involvement of men and women of faith in government is a good thing. Though imperfect, men and women of faith should make an effort to seek wisdom and direction from God to help them abide by principles of justice, charity, honesty, humility and compassion.

Non-partisan prayer for elected officials is a good thing, which is why – as President of the Center for Arizona Policy, a non-partisan pro-family think tank – I hired Guy Chadwick to coordinate and lead prayer activities for governmental leaders in Arizona.

As the Republican nominee for Governor in 2006, I frequently asked for prayer for me and my family, while I personally continued to pray for the Democratic incumbent, Janet Napolitano.

On election night, when I called to congratulate her on her re-election, I told her I would continue to pray for her in the next four years as I had in the previous four.

I was following a worthy example set by Rev. Crutchfield, a partisan Democrat, who prayed for wisdom for all of Arizona's leaders, regardless of party or politics.

I am delighted that Guy Chadwick has undertaken the task of compiling Rev. Crutchfield's prayers. He has also assembled other evidence that Arizona's founding fathers consistently looked to "Almighty God" for provision, for favor and for wisdom.

May this book inspire you to participate in fervent prayer that Arizona's leaders would "find political truth," while working together in a "spirit of conciliation," as we all recognize that God continues to "govern in the affairs of men."

Len Munsil
April 2007

FOREWORD II *by Cheryl Sacks*

America has a rich heritage founded upon prayer. In 1776 the Continental Congress called on the colonies to pray for guidance as they founded a nation. Lincoln bowed on his knees before Gettysburg, and FDR called the nation to prayer on D-Day. Most of us are well aware of the place that prayer to Almighty God has played in the forming of the United States of America.

However, much less is known about God in the foundations of Arizona government. That is the reason I am so pleased that Guy Chadwick has researched and recorded this important subject in the book you now hold in your hands. Perhaps you will be as amazed as I was at how frequently and fervently Arizona's founding fathers publicly declared their reliance upon God and asked for His aid in the forming of Arizona's statehood.

Those of us who petition God regularly for our cities, state, and nation know that current and historical information fuel intercessory prayer. So often this is negative information we receive from daily news. How refreshing it is to discover that the historical foundations of Arizona government are filled with references to God and His Son Jesus Christ.

Reading through *God in the Foundations of Arizona Government* was like opening a treasure chest. Of special interest are the prayers of Chaplain Seaborn Crutchfield and others who asked for Divine Guidance at strategic times and places in Arizona's history. As I journeyed through this book, I found myself stopping to pray in agreement with those who have gone before us. At times, phrases seemed to jump off the page at me— calling out to be prayed again and again.

I hope this book will inspire you to pray for Arizona, too. Even now, why don't you join me in praying one of Chaplain Crutchfield's greatest prayers —"O, Lord!...among the grand galaxy of states in these United States [may] Arizona be the brightest star in the Union."

- Cheryl Sacks, founder, *Arizona Call to Prayer*

– Population Growth History –

The following passage was taken from the prayer given on the first day of the Arizona Constitutional Convention of 1910:

"...Thank God for the circumstances surrounding us today. We pray for guidance that our hearts, hands and tongues may glorify Thy name. We thank Thee for this grand body of sedate men. We trust they are patriots and believe they will frame such a constitution as will bless the teeming thousands that will flow into the state in coming years..."

- *Reverend Seaborn Crutchfield, Convention Chaplain*
Monday, October 10, 1910

The following are historical estimates for our national and state populations based on U.S. census data.

YEAR	UNITED STATES	ARIZONA	AZ as % of U.S.
1863	33 million	~5,000	0.015%
1900	76 million	123,000	0.162%
1910	92 million	204,000	0.222%
1950	151 million	750,000	0.497%
1975	200 million	2.2 million	1.100%
1990	249 million	3.7 million	1.486%
2000	281 million	5.1 million	1.815%
2007	300 million	6.3 million	2.100%

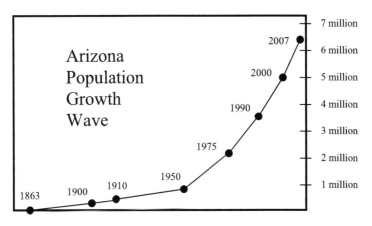

- Preface -

I felt a bit like Forrest Gump. You know— the character that Tom Hanks plays in the movie of the same name where he finds himself unwittingly involved in so many historic moments.

It was January 4, 2007, and I penned my first words for this project while in the original Arizona State Capitol in downtown Phoenix. Simultaneously, in front of the Capitol, our current governor's second-term inauguration ceremony was taking place. I was in the restored third floor House chamber in the very room where the Constitution of the State of Arizona was framed by the Arizona Constitutional Convention of 1910. I was seated at the desk of the President of the Convention, George W. P. Hunt. George Hunt would go on to become the first governor of the state of Arizona and serve a national record seven terms.

Perhaps with a little more intention than the character of Forrest Gump, I chose this historic place and time to inaugurate this work to connect with our state history because I believe the foundations of our history matter.

After spending some time writing at the Convention President's desk I got up to see if I could actually overlook the inauguration ceremony. Sure enough, looking through the blinds of a third story window of another room of the building, I found myself looking directly down upon Governor Napolitano, recently retired U.S. Supreme Court Justice Sandra Day O'Connor, all of the Arizona legislative leadership, the Arizona Supreme Court Justices, and numerous other dignitaries and celebrants. I sincerely hoped that the natural reflection of the window prevented anyone from seeing me positioned as I was above them. I did find out later that my presence there was a serious breach of security even though I had earlier been directed by a Capitol employee to enter a side door inside to the old Capitol.

Having the rather unique role as a prayer coordinator with a special focus on Arizona government, the significance of the moment was not lost on me. Virtually all of the highest-positioned representatives of the three branches of Arizona government were before me. I prayed a simple blessing over each one I recognized, and a general blessing over them all.

The initial inspiration for this project came nearly five years ago with the discovery of the prayers of the first state chaplain, the Reverend Seaborn Crutchfield, recorded verbatim and published in *The Records of the Arizona Constitutional Convention of 1910, Edited by John S. Goff (1991)*. A few of these prayers were first introduced to me by Len Munsil, then President of *The Center for Arizona Policy*. In 2002, I became "*CAP's*" prayer coordinator, the first such paid staff position for a state family policy organization in the nation. This moved me into the governmental arena, and I immediately began to coordinate non-partisan prayer coverage for more than 150 government officials in Arizona. I began to go to the Capitol regularly to pray.

This role as 'governmental prayer' coordinator, in combination with my role as co-director with Cheryl Sacks of *Arizona Call to Prayer*, has provided continual opportunity to see God's mark on Arizona government. Along with other prayer activities, I have led numerous 'intercessory prayer trips' to historic sites throughout Arizona, including to Phoenix, Prescott, Crown King, Navajo Springs, Flagstaff, Tucson, Bisbee, Tombstone, Coronado Memorial, and many other locations. It is fascinating to visit these places in light of their historic significance.

It is my hope that this small effort helps us re-discover and restore Arizona's governmental foundations in God. I know that I have been changed by what I have learned. Upon gaining this understanding, may we better appreciate and build upon the foundation of God in our government. My further hope is that this inspires other works that honor God in a similar way here in Arizona and in other states, for the purpose of more informed prayer and the pursuit of good government.

I. Introduction

"In God we trust" – Our National Motto

America's motto of *"In God we trust"* has its own history that began, like the territory of Arizona, during the Civil War. In the midst of a boon of religious sentiment at the time, a letter of appeal written by Rev. M. R. Watkinson of Pennsylvania to Secretary of the Treasury Salmon P. Chase began the process in 1861. Secretary Chase then instructed the director of the Philadelphia mint to prepare a motto for inclusion on national coins. By 1938 all coins included the motto. In 1956, President Dwight D. Eisenhower approved a Joint Resolution of Congress declaring *"In God we trust"* the official national motto.

What we put in writing, matters. How much more when we inscribe the name of God in a public declaration onto government documents signed by elected representatives of the people? Like our national motto *"IN GOD WE TRUST"* emblazoned on all U.S. currency, when we make such public acknowledgments of the Almighty, I believe it matters to God, and it impacts us for generations.

Though I am unapologetically Christian, my focus is not upon the history of the Church or on religious events *per se,* but to demonstrate, through the straightforward public record, the foundation of God in Arizona government. I will begin with a brief look at our national foundations from which our state was birthed, and then focus on some of the pivotal governmental events and consequent documents that brought Arizona to statehood. I have been amazed to find that time and again God is honored in this written history. What we put in writing, matters.

Israel is a case in point. Her written covenant has always substantiated her foundation with God. Against all odds, we have seen how this covenant has contributed to Israel's existence for generations. As their Torah has been preserved, so has the nation.

Our history recognizes this same God of the Bible. Though we may fail in many respects to live according to His ways, nonetheless we have made clear, written declarations of our dependence upon Him. This helps to determine our standards. This permeates our foundations and forges us into a stream of history based upon Biblical principles for good government.

Mulford Windsor (1874 - 1956) was one of the original delegates of the Arizona Constitutional Convention of 1910 who served multiple terms as an Arizona state senator, and lastly as director of the state library and archives department from 1932 - 1956. He stated in a paper addressed to teachers in 1946:

"The Arizona Constitution did not, any more than the Magna Charta or the Constitution of the United States, fall from the sky, however much of a feeling there may have been in the breasts of many of our people that in view of the boon of statehood which it was presumed to presage it might well be likened to manna from heaven. But it was not a sudden inspiration. It was not spontaneous. It was the culmination of a popular aspiration of long standing." – Mulford Windsor

The framing of our Arizona government did not materialize from nothing, but was built upon the foundations of those who labored beforehand, who, by the grace of God and to our great benefit, acknowledged God and pursued His ways.

I believe these building blocks of governmental record connect us with a transcendent purpose in God—a God Who deeply cares about us and intervenes in our affairs. The better we understand these foundations, the better we can build upon them.

Much of the Old Testament chronicles the course of nations and governments—the battles of kings and armies. A simple word count reveals that the 'nation(s)' and 'kingdom(s)' are mentioned about 1,000 times in the Bible. The words 'king(s)' and 'ruler(s)' are mentioned about 2,500 times! <u>The subject of</u>

government is an undeniably prominent theme throughout the Bible.

> *"O Lord God of our fathers, are You not God in heaven, and do You not rule over all the kingdoms of the nations, and in Your hand is there not power and might, so that no one is able to withstand You?" – 2 Chronicles 20:6*

The New Testament is hardly mute on the subject either. Government, rule, and authority matter very much to God. Here is what the Apostle Paul wrote:

> *"For there is no authority except from God, and the authorities that exist are appointed by God."*
> *– Romans 13:1*

> *"For by Him all things were created that are in heaven and that are on earth, visible and invisible, whether thrones or dominions or principalities or powers. All things were created through Him and for Him."*
> *– Colossians 1:16*

That doesn't leave a lot of wiggle room. According to the Bible, God cares, and He is involved in every aspect of government. This is not the subject of this book, but of all the written documents in history, the Bible has exerted the greatest influence in the shaping of governments in the world today. Its principles underlie every good doctrine of government in the free world. What other written entity could make the same claim?

Let me also offer some of the necessary qualifiers. This project is not about perfect people, nor about the glorifying of Christian men in their roles of shaping our government. Glaring weaknesses and sins could be unearthed regarding virtually every 'Founding Father' of our nation and our state (we all need a Savior for our sins).

This is also not about establishing a Theocracy. The government and the Church are to have distinctive roles in society—not separate, but distinct. It is my observation that many of our misunderstandings on both sides of the debate are the result of confusing these distinctive roles.

The government is to provide executive, judicial, and legislative order, as well as to protect its citizens from harm through a common defense. It is to legislate and enforce the laws of the land—laws that are developed through representative government that <u>protect</u> the weak (but not necessarily provide materially for the weak—that is the role for families and churches) and allow the freest opportunity for life, liberty, and justice for all.

The Church is to bring the good news of Jesus Christ—the message of His atonement for our sins—and to help meet the needs of the poor, afflicted, oppressed, weak, and vulnerable. The Church is to be a "house of prayer" for all people, including first of all for our government authorities (1 Timothy 2:1-4). Christians are also to be salt and light in our culture, and not remove themselves from the public square.

As Len Munsil stated in his Foreword for this book, even unlikely persons at critical times in American history have stood up to acknowledge, even urge, that Christian prayer to "our powerful Friend" is essential to good government.

And God clearly states that He prefers godly government leaders who operate according to Biblical virtues like righteousness, justice, humility, service, and fairness. These government leaders need not be theologians themselves, but it certainly helps when they welcome godly counsel.

God makes provision for the use of imperfect vessels for His 'perfect' work. And it is a process. Isaiah 9:7 says, *"Of the increase of His government and peace there will be no end."* And Jesus taught us to pray in the 'Lord's Prayer'—*"Your kingdom come. Your will be done on earth as it is in heaven."*

If each function—government and the Church—were to fully carry out their role as God intends, problems *would* still occur. We live in a fallen world. But these problems would be attended to more efficaciously without adding to the difficulties. To the degree that government and the Church have been properly aligned, we have prospered. However, when we either mix roles or separate altogether, we only exacerbate our problems.

It is not the separation of Church and State that we need but their *proper* inter-connection that is most beneficial to us all.

Please know that I came to this project not as a scholar, but as a student. Much of the information, especially in the detail and documentation, I learned as I began to write. The research continually opened up areas revealing God's imprint upon our government. And, I know, there is more hidden treasure.

WHAT IS THE PURPOSE OF THIS BOOK?

I began this book with more of an intuitive sense of the need for this information based upon my vantage as a prayer coordinator for the state. The purpose has become clearer as I've progressed.

Psalm 11:3 captures the essence of this assignment: *"If the foundations are destroyed, what can the righteous do?"*

For one, there is a direct application of the principle that historical precedent is important for legal matters. This is an oft-stated fundamental principle of the judicial system, but is also vitally important for many other areas of government.

If we find that Arizona government's original historical precedent incorporates godly principles and the recognition of God Himself, then we have a much stronger legal basis—*authority*—for re-establishing these foundations and building upon them. We would be in a decidedly weaker position should we find this not to be the case, or even if we simply fail to draw on the authority of good historical precedent.

Please note that establishing a sound authority should not provide grounds for arrogance, but all the more requires humility in the character of those in governmental positions as seen in this passage from the prophet Micah:

> *"He has told you, O man, what is good; and what does the Lord require of you but to do justly, to love mercy, and to walk humbly with your God?" – Micah 6:8*

The principle of precedent applies to prayer as well. To the degree that we allow these good foundations to be destroyed, forgotten or buried, we lose our good precedent. When we are able to assert historical precedent in God, we gain authority.

Directly related to the issue of precedent is the important distinction between authority and power. Too often these terms are confused—with potentially degenerative results. Authority is the right to exercise power, but is not power itself. Power may or may not have the proper authority for its exercise. If good government is in effect, then proper authority will restrain unauthorized or wrongly authorized power.

Tragically, when wrong-principled power is allowed to exercise its will, then usually, a new stream of precedent begins. The longer this new stream is allowed to proceed unchecked, the deeper the rut of new precedent. And, it becomes more difficult to return to the original intent. Alas, when the original foundation is so overrun—*what can the righteous do?*

Unrestrained, unauthorized power often tries to intimidate. Whether through the use of brute force or stealth, it hopes that those in authority will acquiesce. <u>A basic strategy used by the enemies of good government has clearly been to destroy the good foundations in order to disarm the proper authorities</u>. This destruction is sometimes attempted by gross denials of the truth and displays of force. Perhaps more frequently, a steady indoctrination process is implemented using language which mocks, discounts, or ignores the good foundations. We see this frequently in the manipulation and pressure exerted by much of the media.

It is one thing to express an opinion, state a case, and attempt to persuade the proper authorities within the boundaries of reporting the truth, or even by presenting a fair and balanced slate of editorials, but quite another for the media to attempt to exercise governmental influence and public persuasion through a biased agenda that consistently perverts the truth.

In summary, the counsel of the first section of Article II of the *Arizona Constitution* written in 1910 is more relevant than ever:

> *"A frequent recurrence to fundamental principles is essential to the security of individual rights and the perpetuity of free government."*

In accordance with this constitutional admonition, I present in this book a review of God in the foundations of Arizona government. I will proceed generally in a chronological order, first with brief discussions on biblical foundations and our national foundations. These are important for the same reason that we need to understand our state foundations—it reveals the unbroken stream of good historical precedent—the recognition of God seen in layer upon layer of the foundations of our government.

Please note that I have included numerous historical quotes throughout this book which I strongly encourage you to read carefully, and not simply skim over. I believe you will find the content of these quotes very interesting and impacting.

"And those from among you will rebuild the ancient ruins;
You will raise up the age-old foundations;
And you will be called the repairer of the breach,
The restorer of the streets in which to dwell."
–Isaiah 58:12

- A Simple Timeline of Our History -

c.1450 BC… Moses receives the Ten Commandments from God
1215 AD… *Magna Charta*, an English contract ("Great Charter")
1492… Christopher (*'Christ-bearer'*) Columbus 'discovers' America
1607… Dedication of land to God at Cape Henry, and first permanent English settlement and church established at Jamestown
1619… First legislative assembly held in the church of Jamestown
1620… *Mayflower Compact*, a New World social contract
1776… Signing of the *Declaration of Independence*
1787… Signing of the *Constitution of the United States of America*
1789… George Washington takes office as our nation's first President
1791… Enacting of the *Bill of Rights* (the first 10 Amendments of the *U. S. Constitution*
1797… President George Washington's Farewell Address
1812 – 1815… War of 1812 against Great Britain and Canada
1848… *Treaty of Guadalupe Hidalgo* secures most of the land of the Southwest for the United States, including most of Arizona, (all of California, Nevada, Utah, and portions of Colorado, Wyoming, and New Mexico)
1853… *The Gadsden Purchase* secures the remaining portions of southern Arizona and southwestern New Mexico
1856… Efforts begin in the pursuit of establishing an Arizona territory
1861 – 1865… *Civil War* between the North and the South
1861 – 1863… A Confederate Arizona territory is organized by the Confederate States of America (with different boundaries)
1863… Feb 24, Abraham Lincoln signs the *Arizona Organic Act* to begin the process of establishing the new Arizona territory
1863… Dec 29, Swearing-in ceremony of the new Arizona territorial government at Navajo Springs, Arizona—John N. Goodwin is the first territorial governor, appointed by President Lincoln
1864… Arizona Capitol first at Fort Whipple, then moved to Prescott
1867… Arizona Capitol moved to Tucson for 10 years
1877… Arizona Capitol moved back to Prescott for 12 years
1889… Arizona Capitol permanently moved to Phoenix
1900… Current Arizona Capitol location opened
1910… June 20, Congress approves the *Enabling Act* for Arizona and New Mexico to hold constitutional conventions for statehood
1910… Oct 10 through Dec 9, *Arizona Constitutional Convention*
1911… Arizona's Constitution is approved by popular vote
1912… Feb 14, President Taft officially signs Arizona into statehood, George W. P. Hunt becomes the first Arizona state governor

II. Biblical Foundations

"That book, Sir, is the Rock upon which our republic rests."
— *President Andrew Jackson, 1845*

As we explore the foundations of our government, we realize that the Bible has provided so much of the inspiration for the tenets of good government, including the concepts of life, liberty, and justice for all. The need for checks and balances in our government are due to the fundamental recognition we have of our fallen 'sin' nature as described in the Bible. The inspiration for our three branches of government—judicial, legislative, and executive—is linked to Isaiah 33:22:

> *"For the Lord is our Judge, the Lord is our Lawgiver, the Lord is our King; He will save us."*

We are a state and nation under God. President Andrew Jackson wrote in reference to the Bible on June 8, 1845, *"That book, Sir, is the Rock upon which our republic rests."*

The principles of righteousness and justice flow from the character of God and His commands as revealed in the Bible. Both Psalm 89:14 and Psalm 97:2 say, *"Righteousness and justice are the foundation of His throne."* Over and over in scripture, and in our public historic documents, God is recognized as the Supreme Being, God Almighty—our ultimate governing authority.

As we lay out this brief historical review of God in the foundations of Arizona government, it is to discover a foundation that not only has historic merit, but consequences for the future. As I mentioned in the Introduction, when we forget God, or even worse, when we intentionally remove God from public recognition, we lose our footing.

However, if we honor and build upon the foundations of God:

*"When the whirlwind passes by, the wicked is no more,
but the righteous has an everlasting foundation."*
– Proverbs 10:25

Jesus himself articulates the distinctive results between building on a good foundation or a bad foundation. Here is Jesus' famous parable of the two foundations:

"Therefore whoever hears these sayings of Mine, and does them, I will liken him to a wise man who built his house on the rock: and the rain descended, the floods came, and the winds blew, and beat on that house; and it did not fall, for it was founded on the rock. But everyone who hears these sayings of Mine, and does not do them, will be like a foolish man who built his house on the sand: and the rain descended, the floods came, and the winds blew and beat on that house; and it fell. And great was its fall." — Matthew 7:24-27

Our foundations are vitally important. Which foundation are we choosing to build upon for our house of government? There are some who are clearly working to destroy the foundations we have in God. However, there are many who are steadfastly committed through prayer, public policy, and good government, to recognize and restore our sound foundations in God.

A few thoughts about Arizona's unique place in our nation...

I believe that Arizona has a specific role in our nation, in part, defined by our place as the "desert state". In the Bible, the wilderness or desert provides a setting for many significant events. Moses, Elijah, and many of the prophets encountered God in the desert. Of course, the nation of Israel wandered 40 years in the desert before coming to the Promised Land. There is the 40 days of fasting and temptation experienced by Jesus in the desert before His ministry was launched. John the Baptist was the voice that *"prepared the way of the Lord"* from the desert. I believe Arizona may carry some of this same destiny for our nation. Could we be a voice *"preparing the way of the Lord?"*

A friend recently noted that Arizona, as the 48th state, was the last to achieve statehood in the contiguous United States—and perhaps the Biblical principle that the *"last shall be first"* may apply to us. Is Arizona to lead the way for our nation regarding some significant new things? Could it be that as we seek and recognize God here in this desert land that we will discover a greater purpose and destiny for Arizona?

THE TEN COMMANDMENTS

I will conclude this brief discussion on Biblical foundations by quoting the Ten Commandments passage in Exodus 20. It is hard to overestimate the influence of the Ten Commandments upon the government and laws of nations.

> *"And God spoke all these words, saying: "I am the Lord your God, who brought you out of the land of Egypt, out of the house of bondage.*
>
> *"You shall have no other gods before Me.*
>
> *"You shall not make for yourself a carved image— any likeness of anything that is in heaven above, or that is in the earth beneath, or that is in the water under the earth; you shall not bow down to them nor serve them. For I, the Lord your God, am a jealous God, visiting the iniquity of the fathers upon the children to the third and fourth generations of those who hate Me, but showing mercy to thousands, to those who love Me and keep My commandments.*
>
> *"You shall not take the name of the Lord your God in vain, for the Lord will not hold him guiltless who takes His name in vain.*
>
> *"Remember the Sabbath day, to keep it holy. Six days you shall labor and do all your work, but the seventh day is the Sabbath of the Lord your God. In it you shall do no work: you, nor your son, nor your daughter, nor your male servant, nor your female servant, nor your cattle, nor your stranger who is within your gates. For in six days the Lord made the heavens and the earth, the sea, and all that is in them, and rested on the seventh day.*

Therefore, the Lord blessed the Sabbath day and hallowed it.

"Honor your father and your mother, that your days may be long upon the land which the Lord your God is giving you.

"You shall not murder.

"You shall not commit adultery.

"You shall not steal.

"You shall not bear false witness against your neighbor.

"You shall not covet your neighbor's house; you shall not covet your neighbor's wife, nor his male servant, nor his female servant, nor his ox, nor his donkey, nor anything that is your neighbor's.""

— *Exodus 20:1-17*

Moses and the Ten Commandments by Rembrandt – 1659

III. Our National Foundations

"Blessed is the nation whose God is the Lord" – Psalm 33:12

Thankfully, in recent years there has been a great resurgence of scholarship confirming the Christian heritage of our nation. I will note some highlights and mention a list of resources.

David Barton and the *Wallbuilders* ministry chronicle thousands of historic documents, references, biographies and events proving beyond any doubt, despite some revisionists' attempts to the contrary, that our nation has deep, fundamentally Christian roots (see the website: www.wallbuilders.com).

America's God and Country (1999) by William J. Federer is an encyclopedia of thousands of quotations by our Founding Fathers, Presidents, statesmen, scientists, constitutions, Supreme Court justices, and other leaders. This resource reassures us with the record of so many who shaped our nation with their avowed dependence on the Bible and their Christian faith.

Even so, it is important to clarify what determines a nation's status as Christian. As clarified by *America's Providential History*, by Mark Beliles and Stephen McDowell (1989):

> *"What makes America a Christian nation? Many Christians erroneously believe it depends on whether or not our Founders were Christians. Others believe it depends on if a vast majority of Americans are Christians. The problem with these criteria is when one or more of our Founders are found not to be Christians; does that negate the rest? ...Does the fallibility of Christians in a Christian nation negate the claim? Of course not... A Christian nation is determined by its **form** of government, not who formed it. If the form of a nation's government is shaped by Biblical ideas of man and government, in contrast to pagan or man centered ideas, then the nation is a Christian nation... Our Founders were universally convinced of this truth."* — *p.185*

This, of course, does not deny the importance of having such a rich heritage of those who are professed Christians. First, there is the practical reason that a form of Christian-principled government is highly unlikely without Christians inspired by their faith to frame it.

Second, the exercise of any form of government certainly stands a better chance of success when carried out by godly government leaders with the well-being of all citizens in mind. On October 11, 1798, President John Adams stated in his address to the military (*America's God and Country,* p. 10-11):

> *"We have no government armed with power capable of contending with human passions unbridled by morality and religion. Avarice, ambition, revenge, or gallantry, would break the strongest cords of our Constitution as a whale goes through a net. Our Constitution was made only for a moral and religious people. It is wholly inadequate to the government of any other."*

On October 12, 1816, our first Chief Justice of the U.S. Supreme Court, John Jay, appointed by President George Washington, stated in a correspondence (*America's God and Country,* p. 318):

> *"<u>Providence has given to our people the choice of their rulers, and it is the duty, as well as the privilege and interest of our Christian nation, to select and prefer Christians for their rulers.</u>"*

MAGNA CARTA - 1215

Historical reviews consistently point to the Magna Carta as a key source document leading to American government. As Alan Crippen stated in his paper, <u>*British Christianity and the American Order – Stephen Langton and the Magna Carta*</u> (2006), *"First of all, it acknowledges that the king reigns by God's grace... there is a law that is higher than the state's. It is God's law, and the implication is that the King is accountable to a rule of law that transcends the state."*

Translated from the original Latin of the *Magna Carta* (or Charta) of England, which means "Great Charter" or literally "Great Papers", first written in 1215, it begins this way:

> *"John, <u>by the grace of God</u>, King of England... <u>know that before God</u>, for the health of our soul and those of our ancestors and heirs, <u>to the honour of God</u>, the exaltation of the holy Church, and the better ordering of our kingdom... First, <u>that we have granted to God</u>, and by this present charter have confirmed for us and our heirs in perpetuity, that the English Church shall be free, and shall have its rights undiminished, and its liberties unimpaired... Since <u>we have granted all these things for God</u>, for the better ordering of our kingdom, and to allay the discord that has arisen between us..."*

Crippen also comments in regard to the distinction of the roles of church and state as reflected in the Magna Carta:

> *"The totalizing tendency of the state was to be held in check by the prophetic voice of the Church... The Church was to order the soul. The state was to order society. Both institutions were to foster and facilitate the commonwealth. Without the order of the soul, there could be no political order in and of the commonwealth."*

JAMESTOWN - 1607

Jamestown in 1607 builds on the English standard of acknowledging God, as seen in the First Charter of Virginia issued by King James I of England for the Virginia Company:

> *"We, greatly commending and graciously accepting of their Desires for the Furtherance of so noble a Work, which may, <u>by the Providence of Almighty God, hereafter tend to the Glory of His Divine Majesty</u>, in propagating of Christian Religion to such People, as yet live in Darkness and miserable Ignorance of the true Knowledge and Worship of God..."*

The Virginia Company first reached America on April 26, 1607. However, the company's chaplain, Rev. Robert Hunt, had them wait in their ships for 3 days of prayer and fasting to better prepare their hearts. The company then landed at Cape Henry, planted a tall white wooden cross in the sand, and prayed and dedicated the land to God. The company then navigated further inland to establish Jamestown and the first church. In 1619, they were commissioned to hold the first legislative government assembly of the New World in that church.

THE MAYFLOWER COMPACT - 1620

A year and a half later, on November 11, 1620, the Pilgrims arrived in New England, with the *Mayflower Compact* in hand:

The Mayflower Compact, from the journal of William Bradford

"In ye name of God, Amen. We whose names are underwritten, the loyall subjects of our dread soveraigne Lord, King James, by ye grace of God, of Great Britaine, Franc, & Ireland king, defender of ye faith, &c., having undertaken, for ye glorie of God, and advancement of ye Christian faith, and honour of our king & countrie, a

voyage to plant ye first colonie in ye Northerne parts of Virginia, doe by these presents solemnly & mutually in ye presence of God, and one another, covenant & combine our selves together into a civill body politick, for our better ordering & preservation & furtherance of ye ends aforesaid; and by virtue hearof to enacte, constitute, and frame such just & equall laws, ordinances, acts, constitutions, & offices, from time to time, as shall be thought most meete & convenient for ye generall good of ye Colonie, unto which we promise all due submission and obedience. In witness wherof we have hereunder subscribed our names at Cape Codd..."

Drafted by the Pilgrims as they crossed the Atlantic in the *Mayflower*, the *Mayflower Compact* provided the first governing social contract of the New World for the Plymouth Colony. Some of the language of the *Magna Carta* is evident, which preceded the *Compact* by 400 years.

DECLARATION OF INDEPENDENCE - 1776

Moving forward to the birth of our nation, the *Declaration of Independence* of July 4, 1776, includes these famous statements:

"We hold these truths to be self-evident, that all men are created equal. That they are endowed by their Creator with certain inalienable Rights, that among these are Life, Liberty, and the Pursuit of Happiness..."

"We, therefore, the Representatives of the United States of America, in General Congress, Assembled, appealing to the Supreme Judge of the world for the rectitude of our intentions, do..."

"And for the support of this Declaration, with a firm Reliance on the Protection of divine Providence, we mutually pledge to each other our Lives, our Fortunes, and our sacred Honor...

U.S. CONSTITUTION & BILL OF RIGHTS – 1787 & 1791

The *Constitution of the United States of America* (1787) and the subsequent *Bill of Rights* in 1791 (the first 10 Amendments) further set forth the Christian principles of life, liberty, and justice for all, checks and balances in government, and a government structure validated only by the consent of the governed. These build on the foundation of such documents as the *Magna Carta* and the *Mayflower Compact* and the collective wisdom of a truly remarkable council of predominantly Christian men—our nation's Founding Fathers.

First page of the U.S. Constitution – 1787

For a scholarly documentary history of the *U.S. Constitution* and *Bill of Rights,* I point you to *Sources of Our Liberties*, edited by Richard L. Perry and John C. Cooper published by the American Bar Foundation in 1978. Beginning with the *Magna Carta*, this book reviews some thirty charters and constitutions of England

and the New World that formed the basis for the *U.S. Constitution* and *Bill of Rights*. Many of these charters include clear references to God and recognition of Christian fundamentals.

For example, the Pennsylvania Charter of Privileges of October 28, 1701, written by William Penn, "Proprietary and Governor of the Province of Pensilvania," states in the "FIRST" section of his charter (*Sources of Our Liberties,* p. 256):

"BECAUSE no People can be truly happy, though under the greatest Enjoyment of Civil Liberties, if abridged of the Freedom of their Consciences, as to their Religious Profession and Worship: <u>And Almighty God being the only Lord of Conscience, Father of Lights and Spirits; and the Author as well as Object of all divine Knowledge, Faith and Worship, who only doth enlighten the Minds, and persuade and convince the Understandings of People</u>, I do hereby grant and declare, That no Person or Persons, inhabiting in this Province or Territories, who shall confess and acknowledge One almighty God, the Creator, Upholder and Ruler of the World; and profess him or themselves obliged to live quietly under the Civil Government, shall be in any Case molested or prejudiced, in his or their Person or Estate, because of his or their conscientious Persuasion or Practice, nor be compelled to frequent or maintain any religious Worship, Place or Ministry, contrary to his or their Mind, or to do or suffer any other Act or Thing, contrary to their religious Persuasion.

"AND that all Persons who also profess to believe in Jesus Christ, the Saviour of the World, shall be capable (notwithstanding their other Persuasions and Practices in Point of Conscience and Religion) to serve this Government in any Capacity, both legislatively and executively..."

As we see over and again, there is a consistent recognition of God in the stream of these historic documents.

In light of this overwhelming evidence that is so readily linked to the fact that we are the freest and most prosperous nation in history, it is remarkable why this heritage would be ignored in so many influential circles today. There are no prominent references of any other faith shaping our American government history. Our Christian foundation in God is what makes us who we are.

Our sixth U.S. President, John Quincy Adams, issued the following statements in speeches on the 45th and 61st anniversaries of July 4th Independence Day celebrations (*America's God and Country, p.18*):

> *"The highest glory of the American Revolution was this: <u>it connected, in one indissoluble bond, the principles of civil government with the principles of Christianity.</u>"*
> —July 4, 1821

> *"Why is it that next to the birthday of the Savior of the World, your most joyous and most venerated festival returns on this day. Is it not that, in the chain of human events, the birthday of the nation is indissolubly linked with the birthday of the Savior? That it forms a leading event in the Progress of the Gospel dispensation? Is it not that the Declaration of Independence first organized the social compact on the foundation of the Redeemer's mission upon earth? That it laid the cornerstone of human government upon the first precepts of Christianity and gave to the world the first irrevocable pledge of the fulfillment of the prophecies announced directly from Heaven at the birth of the Savior and predicted by the greatest of the Hebrew prophets 600 years before."*
> —July 4, 1837

These are not the words of clergy, but of a U.S. President.

<u>It is also noteworthy that all 50 state constitutions acknowledge God</u> (see the complete listing on pp. 138-143).

PROCLAMATIONS OF DAYS OF PRAYER & FASTING

Another very telling witness of America's written declarations of God are the numerous public proclamations for days of prayer and fasting issued by government leaders, including Presidents, Congress, Governors, and military leaders. They were often referred to as a "Proclamation for a Day of Prayer and Humiliation." One such particularly moving proclamation was issued by President Abraham Lincoln on March 30, 1863 (*America's God and Country*, p. 383-384). This proclamation was issued just a few weeks after he signed the *Arizona Organic Act* which birthed the new Arizona Territory.

President Abraham Lincoln (1809-1865), photo: 1861
Issuer of the Emancipation Proclamation – January 1, 1863
Signer of the Arizona Organic Act – February 24, 1863

"Whereas, the Senate of the United States devoutly recognizing the Supreme Authority and just Government of Almighty God in all the affairs of men and of nations, has, by a resolution, requested the President to designate and set apart a day for national prayer and humiliation:

And whereas, it is the duty of nations as well as of men to own their dependence upon the overruling power of God, to confess their sins and transgressions in humble sorrow yet with assured hope that genuine repentance will lead to mercy and pardon, and to recognize the sublime truth, announced in the Holy Scriptures and proven by all history: that those nations are blessed whose God is the Lord:

And, insomuch as we know that, by His divine law, nations like individuals are subjected to punishments and chastisement in this world, may we not justly fear that the awful calamity of civil war, which now desolates the land may be but a punishment inflicted upon us for our presumptuous sins to the needful end of our national reformation as a whole people?

We have been the recipients of the choicest bounties of Heaven. We have been preserved these many years in peace and prosperity. We have grown in numbers, wealth and power as no other nation has ever grown.

But we have forgotten God. We have forgotten the gracious Hand which preserved us in peace, and multiplied and enriched and strengthened us; and we have vainly imagined, in the deceitfulness of our hearts, that all these blessings were produced by some superior wisdom and virtue of our own.

Intoxicated with unbroken success, we have become too self-sufficient to feel the necessity of redeeming and preserving grace, too proud to pray to the God that made us!

It behooves us then to humble ourselves before the offended Power, to confess our national sins and to pray for clemency and forgiveness.

Now, therefore, in compliance with the request and fully concurring in the view of the Senate, I do, by this my proclamation, designate and set apart Thursday, the 30th of April, 1863, as a day of national humiliation, fasting and prayer.

And I do hereby request all the people to abstain on that day from their ordinary secular pursuits, and to unite, at their several places of public worship and their respective homes, in keeping the day holy to the Lord and devoted to the humble discharge of the religious duties proper to that solemn occasion.

All this being done, in sincerity and truth, let us then rest humbly in the hope authorized by the Divine teachings, that the united cry of the nation will be heard on high and answered with blessings no less than the pardon of our national sins and the restoration of our now divided and suffering country to its former happy condition of unity and peace."

In witness whereof, I have hereunto set my hand and caused the seal of the United States to be affixed. By the President:

Abraham Lincoln

APPOINTMENT OF CHAPLAINS

The chaplaincy has been an integral part of American history – from Jamestown in 1607, throughout the military conflicts of the 17th and 18th centuries, and then formally established by an act of the Continental Congress in 1775. One of the first acts of Congress was to appoint paid chaplains for the government, whose duties included opening every legislative session in prayer and serving the legislators' needs. This protocol continues to this day for legislative bodies across America.

CONCLUSION ON THE NATIONAL FOUNDATIONS

The next chapter will discuss the key treaties that brought the land of Arizona into U.S. possession. First, I would like to conclude this brief review of our national foundations in God by referring to President George Washington, who was a descendent of King John of England, and of English Barons directly connected with the Magna Carta (*America's God and Country*, p. 635). With his hand upon an open Bible, on April 30, 1789, he took his first oath of office on the balcony of Federal Hall in New York City. Here are quotes from our first President (from *America's God and Country*):

> "*...it would be peculiarly improper to omit, in this first official act, my fervent supplications to that Almighty Being who rules over the universe, who presides in the councils of nations and whose providential aids can supply every human defect, that His benediction may consecrate to the liberties and happiness of the people of the United States a Government instituted by themselves for these essential purposes... In tendering this homage to the Great Author of every public and private good... No people can be bound to acknowledge and adore the Invisible Hand which conducts the affairs of men more than the people of the United States. Every step by which they have advanced to the character of an independent nation seems to have been distinguished by some token of providential agency... We ought to be no less persuaded that the propitious smiles of Heaven can*

<u>never be expected on a nation that disregards the eternal rules of order and right which Heaven itself has ordained</u>... the Benign Parent of the Human Race...has been pleased to favor the American people with opportunities for deliberating in perfect tranquility, and dispositions for deciding with unparalleled unanimity on a form of government for the security of the union and the advancement of their happiness, so His divine blessings may be equally conspicuous in the enlarged views, the temperate consultations and the wise measures on which the success of this Government must depend..." (from Washington's first Inaugural address, 1789, p. 651-652)

"It is impossible to rightly govern the world without God and the Bible."—attributed to George Washington (p. 660)

"Of all the dispositions and habits which lead to political prosperity, Religion and morality are indispensible supports... <u>Who... can look with indifference upon attempts to shake the foundation of the fabric?</u>" (from Washington's Farewell Address, 1797, p. 661)

The 1797 Gilbert Stuart portrait of President George Washington

IV. The Treaties to Secure the Land of Arizona

"In the Name of Almighty God..."

1. TREATY OF GUADALUPE HIDALGO - 1848

"Under the Protection of Almighty God, the Author of Peace..."

We now advance 50 years following George Washington's *Farewell Address*, to the *Treaty of Guadalupe Hidalgo*. This treaty set the stage for the birth of Arizona by bringing most of the Southwest into the possession of the United States. The treaty was signed on February 2, 1848 in the city of Guadalupe Hidalgo near Mexico City. It ended the *Mexican-American War* which had officially begun on May 13, 1846, and had erupted as part of on-going clashes since the 1830s, primarily surrounding disputes concerning the territory of Texas.

The treaty resulted in 525,000 square miles of land being ceded to the United States, then some 55% of Mexico's territory, for $15 million and the agreement to take over $3.25 million in debts Mexico owed to American citizens. This land included virtually all of what would become California, Nevada, and Utah, portions of Colorado, Wyoming, New Mexico, and most of Arizona.

Along with the extreme historic consequence of this treaty in terms of land acquisition for the United States (see the following map), again this document prominently honors God. Below is the beginning of the document, which contains 23 Articles that define borders, troop withdrawal, financial terms, etc.

Treaty of Guadalupe Hidalgo; February 2, 1848

Treaty of Peace, Friendship, Limits, and Settlement between the United States of America and the United Mexican States concluded at Guadalupe Hidalgo,

February 2, 1848; Ratification advised by Senate, with Amendments, March 10, 1848; Ratified by President, March 16, 1848; Ratifications Exchanged at Queretaro, May 30, 1848; Proclaimed, July 4, 1848.

IN THE NAME OF ALMIGHTY GOD:

*The United States of America and the United Mexican States animated by a sincere desire to put an end to the calamities of the war which unhappily exists between the two Republics and to establish Upon a solid basis relations of peace and friendship, which shall confer reciprocal benefits upon the citizens of both, and assure the concord, harmony, and mutual confidence wherein the two people should live, as good neighbors have for that purpose appointed their respective plenipotentiaries, that is to say: The President of the United States has appointed Nicholas P. Trist, a citizen of the United States, and the President of the Mexican Republic has appointed Don Luis Gonzaga Cuevas, Don Bernardo Couto, and Don Miguel Atristain, citizens of the said Republic; Who, after a reciprocal communication of their respective full powers, have, **under the protection of Almighty God, the author of peace,** arranged, agreed upon, and signed the following: Treaty of Peace, Friendship, Limits, and Settlement between the United States of America and the Mexican Republic.*

ARTICLE I

There shall be firm and universal peace between the United States of America and the Mexican Republic, and between their respective countries, territories, cities, towns, and people, without exception of places or persons.

The phrases, *"In the Name of Almighty God,"* the introductory heading of the treaty, and *"under the protection of Almighty God, the author of peace"* in the opening statement or preamble of the treaty, are notably significant mutual national agreements on the overriding authority of God. To put it another way, the acknowledgments of God are not a part of the small print!

2. THE GADSDEN PURCHASE – 1853

"In the Name of Almighty God"

The Gadsden Purchase of 1853 completed the land acquisitions for the contiguous United States, securing what would become southern Arizona and southwestern New Mexico for $10 million. Signed by President Franklin Pierce, the primary purpose of this treaty was to make available land to build a southern transcontinental railroad, and also to better compensate Mexico in light of what was commonly considered to be a relatively small payment made for all the land acquired by the *Treaty of Guadalupe Hidalgo*.

BY THE PRESIDENT OF
THE UNITED STATES OF AMERICA

A PROCLAMATION.

WHEREAS a treaty between the United States of America and the Mexican Republic was concluded and signed at the City of Mexico on the thirtieth day of December, one thousand eight hundred and fifty-three; which treaty, as amended by the Senate of the United States, and being in the English and Spanish languages, is word for word as follows:

IN THE NAME OF ALMIGHTY GOD:

The Republic of Mexico and the United States of America desiring to remove every cause of disagreement which might interfere in any manner with the better friendship and intercourse between the two countries, and especially in respect to the true limits which should be established, when, notwithstanding what was covenanted in the treaty of Guadalupe Hidalgo in the year 1848, opposite interpretations have been urged, which might give occasion to questions of serious moment: to avoid these, and to strengthen and more firmly maintain the peace which happily prevails between the two republics, the President of the United States has, for this purpose, appointed James Gadsden...

The Gadsden Purchase, with its nine articles, further clarified border lines and transportation issues between Mexico and the United States. With this complete, the land was secured *"in the name of Almighty God"* which would soon become the Territory of Arizona.

A MAP OF THE LAND ACQUISITIONS GAINED BY THE TREATY OF GUADALUPE HIDALGO OF 1848 AND THE GADSDEN PURCHASE OF 1853

Courtesy of Wikipedia, the free on-line encyclopedia

V. New Arizona Territory - 1863

Battle Cry of Freedom
Words & Music by George F. Root, 1862

Yes we rally 'round the flag, boys, we'll rally once again,
Shouting the battle cry of Freedom,
We will rally from the hillside, we'll gather from the plain,
Shouting the battle cry of Freedom.

We are springing to the call of our brothers gone before,
Shouting the battle cry of Freedom,
And we'll fill the vacant ranks with a million Free men more,
Shouting the battle cry of Freedom.

These are the first two verses of what was considered the most popular rallying song of the Union. It was also sung as part of the ceremony of the official organization of the Arizona territorial government at Navajo Springs on December 29, 1863.

After the *Gadsden Purchase*, the next ten years saw the brewing conflict of slavery develop into the Civil War. Meanwhile the western desert region focused primarily on mining exploration which was made difficult by the harsh conditions and often hostile and poorly understood relationships with some of the Native American tribes in the area.

Leading up to the *Arizona Organic Act*, which was signed by President Abraham Lincoln on February 24, 1863, there were several attempts to gain territorial status, even as early as 1856. However, the population was considered too small to warrant official territorial status and the growing conflict between the North and South carried into a corresponding rift between the northern and southern delegates in Congress.

The control of Arizona was important as a land bridge to California. Indeed, in 1861, the Confederate States of America, under President Jefferson Davis, seceded from the Union and formed a Confederate Arizona Territory, using borders that incorporated what is now the southern halves of New Mexico and Arizona, officially enacted on February 14, 1862, exactly fifty years prior to Arizona statehood. This lasted for one year until Congress, now without the southern delegates, enacted the *Arizona Organic Act* with President Lincoln's signature.

The new United States Territory of Arizona re-defined our boundaries to those of the present, with one exception. A final border change occurred by an act of Congress in 1866. This act took a portion of northwestern Arizona territory—"the lost county"—and gave it to Nevada.

Before starting westward in order to set up the government in the new Arizona Territory, the officials sat for this portrait in 1863. From left to right are: Henry W. Fleury, the Governor's private secretary; Associate Justice Joseph P. Allyn, U.S. Marshal Milton B. Duffield, Governor John Goodwin, U.S. District Attorney Almon P. Gage, and Richard C. McCormick, Secretary of the Arizona Territory. By permission of the Arizona Historical Foundation.

By law, U.S. territorial government officials were to be appointed by the President of the United States, and thus Abraham Lincoln appointed the first territorial government officials of Arizona. The plan was for the governmental party to reach Fort Whipple, near present-day Prescott, on Christmas Day of 1863, and establish the new Arizona government there. Due to various travel delays, this would not happen, and resulted in the story of Navajo Springs.

After months of preparations and some adjustments to the appointments of officials, the Arizona territorial government party, including a military escort to guard against Confederate and Apache attack, was able to set out on October 15, 1863 from Ft. Larnard (Larned) in Nebraska. After more delays, the wagon train arrived at Navajo Springs just inside the new Arizona Territory on December 29, 1863. The government party had just crossed over the line from New Mexico, and therefore they were eligible to swear in the first territorial officers whose appointments would lapse at the end of the year. They knew they would not reach Fort Whipple for about three weeks, and with no known watering places available for the next several days travel, this was deemed the best place to stop and hold the swearing in ceremony before the year ran out.

Thus, at 4:00pm on December 29, 1863, the government party assembled. The 'Stars and Stripes' were raised, the oaths of office for the new territorial governor, John N. Goodwin, territorial secretary, Richard C. McCormick, three judges, and other government officials were administered. An invocation was given by Reverend Hiram Walker Read. The written proclamation of the territorial government was spoken. Thus, at this otherwise obscure watering place was the new Arizona government established on a cold and windy afternoon in a largely treeless and barren high desert in northeastern Arizona—now hidden away in Navajo Nation land.

Excerpts from letters of a member of the Arizona governmental party of 1863 provide more historical insight into the governmental parties' travels:

From the letters of Jonathan Richmond, a member of Governor Goodwin's governmental party from the *History of Arizona* p. 65-70, by Thomas Edwin Farish, Arizona Historian, Volume 3, Phoenix, Arizona, 1916, from the on-line *Books of the Southwest* collection of the University of Arizona Library:

"Navajo Springs, Arizona,"Dec. 29th, 1863.

"Dear Parents:"<u>We arrived here today, and the Governor has issued his proclamation, a copy of which I enclose. This is the first point Which we know is in Arizona Territory</u>. I bought me a burro (jackass) at Zuni. Shall not reach Fort Whipple before January 20th, 1864. Will write at length on our arrival. This goes to Wingate by military express (one of our soldiers), in the morning. All well. Love to all.

"Your son,"JONATHAN."

"Fort Whipple, Arizona,"Jany. 27th, 1864.

"Dear Parents:"<u>Our arrival here was announced by the firing of a Governor's salute of eighteen guns on the morning of the 22nd. Offers of prayers and thanksgiving should have been made</u>, but upon viewing the site which Major Willis, (who, with three companies, preceded us two weeks) had selected for a military post, and, if suitable, for a capitol, we concluded to let the thing slide. We are located about two hundred and sixty miles northwest of Tucson, and about ninety miles west of the San Francisco mountains on a small stream of water supposed to be, and, for the present, called the head Waters of the San Francisco river. The climate is mild as in the States in June. We all go about in our shirt sleeves during the day, but at sundown an overcoat is very comfortable...

Note the line: *"offers of prayers and thanksgivings should have been made..."* Though I would like to report that our first government was diligent in every instance to dedicate significant events to God, at least it is interesting to note that by this very admission it further substantiates the common practice of honoring God in that day. His letters continue…

"The mines are twenty-five miles from here, but there are a few cabins eighteen miles. The Antelope Diggings are sixty miles, all on the Tucson road. There are some who have very rich claims, but the want of water prevents their working them at present. Large tanks are being made on the summit of the mountain to be ready for the spring rains. Morehouse, brother of B. & F., who are with us, arrived yesterday from Tucson. He takes Mr. Wrightson's goods and with the boys proceeds to the Santa Rita mines. He has specimens of gold which he picked out with his knife while on his way up.

"On our arrival we noticed several individuals who were very anxious to form the acquaintance of the officials and others of the party, and who are now known as being candidates for Delegate to Congress. There are some twenty or more now at Tucson who make no bones of the wished for position. Most of the candidates, I understand, are from California.

"The outfit for the present (probably two months) remains here. The Governor, with a party, Start on an expedition with pack mules in search of a site for the capitol the first of the week. They will go down on the Salinas river and from there west to the Colorado. Judge Howell goes at the earliest opportunity to Tucson, where, it is said, business is awaiting him. I go into the mines on Monday, packing my jackass with a month's provisions, thinking by that time to be able to judge whether mining will pay. I may go to Tucson during the term of court which will be in March. On the 19th inst., B. Morehouse and myself, with several Mexicans, had a fight with a party of Tonto Apaches, killing two on the spot, and wounding two so badly that they are probably dead before this. Judge says he intends writing the "Eagle" on the fight.

"Write! Write!! Write!!! care of Governor Goodwin, Fort Whipple, Arizona Territory. Love to all.

Your son, "JONATHAN."

Jonathan Richmond then recounts the ceremony and activities of Navajo Springs in more detail upon arriving at Fort Whipple a few weeks later (he had complained about not having a good place to write on the day of the occasion, and had perhaps been too engaged in the care of his new burro):

"The officers entered the Territory on the 27th of December, and the government was formally inaugurated at Navajo Springs, 40 miles west of Zuni [New Mexico], on Tuesday the 29th of December. At 4 o'clock p. m. the escort and citizens were assembled, and Secretary McCormick spoke as follows:

"Gentlemen:—As the properly qualified officer, it becomes my duty to inaugurate the proceedings of the day. After a long and trying journey, we have arrived within the limits of the Territory of Arizona. These broad plains and hills form a part of the district over which, as the representatives of the United States, we are to establish a civil government. Happily, although claimed by those now in hostility to the Federal arms, we take possession of the Territory without resort to military force. The flag, which I hoist in token of our authority, is no new and untried banner. For nearly a century it has been the recognized, the honored, the loved emblem of law and liberty. From Canada to Mexico, from the Atlantic to the Pacific millions of strong arms are raised in its defense, and above the efforts of all foreign or domestic foes, it is destined to live untarnished and transcendent."

"At the conclusion of these remarks, Mr. McCormick hoisted the "Stars and Stripes" and called for cheers for them, which were given with a will. Prayer was then offered by the Rev. H. W. Read. The oath of office was administered to Chief Justice Turner, and to Associate Justices Howell, and Allyn, by Mr. McCormick. Governor Goodwin and District Attorney Gage qualified before Chief Justice Turner.

"A proclamation by the Governor, which is here reproduced, was read in English by Mr. McCormick, and in Spanish by Mr. Read.

"Fort Whipple had been established a month previous to the arrival of the Territorial officers, by Major E. B. Willis, of the First California Infantry, under the order of Brigadier-General James H. Carleton, commanding the Military Department of New Mexico..."

The transcription of the proclamation, which was read in English and Spanish on December 29, 1863, is as follows:

PROCLAMATION.
TO THE PEOPLE OF ARIZONA:

I, JOHN N. GOODWIN, having been appointed by the President of the United States, and duly qualified, as Governor of the TERRITORY OF ARIZONA, do hereby announce that by virtue of the powers with which I am invested by an Act of the Congress of the United States, providing a temporary government for the Territory, I shall this day proceed to organize said government. The provisions of the Act, and all laws and enactments established thereby, will be enforced by the proper Territorial officers from and after this date.

A preliminary census will forthwith be taken, and thereafter the Judicial Districts will be formed, and an election of members of the Legislative Assembly, and the other officers, provided by the Act, be ordered.

I invoke the aid and co-operation of all citizens of the Territory in my efforts to establish a government whereby the security of life and property will be maintained throughout its limits, and its varied resources be rapidly and successfully developed.

The seat of government will for the present be at or near Fort Whipple.

JOHN N. GOODWIN

By the Governor:
RICHARD C. M'CORMICK,
Secretary of the Territory
Navajo Springs, ARIZONA,
December 29, 1863.

There is no known verbatim record of the dedicatory prayer given by the Reverend Hiram W. Read at the Navajo Springs ceremony.

NOTE: For a detailed account of our 'intercessory prayer journey' to the site of Navajo Springs by a team of twelve on February 18, 2006 see the Appendix, p 167-173. It may be that we were the first to pray at the original place of Arizona government since the 1863 event!

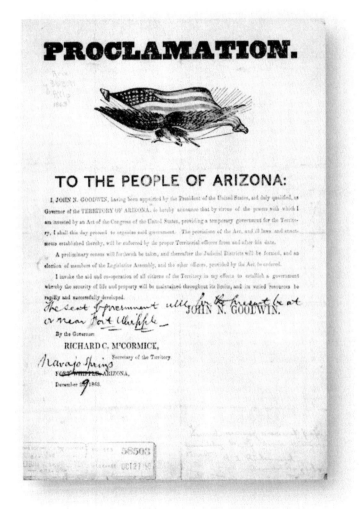

Copy of the original proclamation – at the Arizona Capitol Archives Courtesy of the Arizona State Library, Archives and Public Records

Following the Navajo Springs event which 'organized' the government, the government party reached Fort Whipple on January 22, 1864. At first they lived in tents at the Fort while they began to survey and build at the site nearby which would become Prescott. They established the capitol there later that year. Tucson laid claim that it deserved to be the capital city with its longer history and greater population base in the territory. However, the Civil War still raged on and too many Confederate sympathizers were located in Tucson and southern Arizona for the northern-appointed government officials.

Monument marking the 'organizing' of the Arizona Territorial government at Navajo Springs on December 29, 1863, photo by Rose Ann Tompkins, 2001.

The preceding photograph and additional historical references for Navajo Springs, are available on a website by Tom Jonas at: www.tomjonas.com/swex/navajosprings.

THE FIRST ARIZONA TERRITORIAL LEGISLATURE

"May the Supreme Law-giver of the universe… give us wisdom"
- John N. Goodwin, first Territorial Governor of Arizona, 1864

The first legislative assembly of the new Arizona Territory was originally convened in Prescott on September 26, 1864, but due to various absences, only adjourned the first three days until opening a full session on September 29. The first legislative assembly continued until November 9, 1864.

One of the first orders of business was a motion to appoint a Chaplain of the Council, which failed, but then resulted in the following action:

"Resolved, by the Council, the House of Representatives concurring, That the Rev. H. W. Read [the same who attended the governmental party travels to Arizona and gave the invocation at Navajo Springs] be invited to hold divine service in this building each Sabbath during the session of the Legislature." (p. 94, Vol. III, History of Arizona)

Thus, in a curious twist on Jamestown history—where the first legislative assembly of the nation met in a church building in 1619—in Prescott the first assembly of Arizona invited the church to meet in its building!

In fact, later in the assembly, on October 21, 1864, Henry W. Fleury, who was Governor Goodwin's private secretary, was elected as the Chaplain of the body, and then Chaplain of the Council. Interesting— Mr. Fleury served both as Chaplain and private secretary to the highest governmental authority in Arizona.

To conclude the first legislative day of the first legislative assembly on September 29, the Governor gave a lengthy speech which explained the need for a new system of laws, and reviewed the circumstances and challenges they faced in the new, raw territory, and the responsibility they had to establish good government for the prosperity of all Arizona citizens.

Here are some excerpts from Goodwin's opening-day speech:

"As the representatives of the people of Arizona, elected in accordance with the provisions of its organic law, you are this day convened in Legislative Assembly.

Accept my congratulations, that with the organization of your body the territorial government is inaugurated in all its branches and rests on the foundation of the will and power of the people. The law... provides that 'the legislative power and authority shall be vested in the Legislative Assembly, and the Governor, and shall extend to all rightful subjects of legislation, consistent with its provisions and the constitution of the United States; and all laws passed by them shall be binding unless disapproved by Congress.'

"Power so great, authority so unlimited, involves equal responsibility.

"And we must be impressed with a full sense of the stern and delicate duty confided to us, when we consider the importance and grandeur of the work we are selected to perform.

"<u>We are here, clothed with the power to make laws which may forever shape the destiny of this territory, to lay the foundations of a new state, and to build up a new commonwealth</u>. The consequences of our official acts are not within our control, nor can we escape them.

"There record either to our glory or shame will soon be made, and impartial history will render a verdict, from which there is no appeal. It is in our power by wise, just, and liberal legislation, to advance this territory far onward in the race for empire; or by regarding only the selfish promptings of the present, and ignoring the logic of events, forgetting the teachings of the past, and the grand anticipations of the future, to impede its prosperity and retard its progress. We are entrusted not only with the present interests of a small constituency, and amenable to them alone, but we are the trustees of posterity, and responsible to the millions who in all time shall come after us. The saints and martyrs of liberty, who founded the Republic, have given us in trust the greatest blessings that can be bestowed upon men—civil and religious liberty—it is our duty as legislators to transmit this gift to our successors unimpaired. The constitution of the United States, which is the ark of our liberties, and the organic

law giving vitality to our acts, are the guides and limits to our legislation.

"Happily for our action there is abundant precedent. We have the teachings of the fathers, and can follow in the way marked out by the men of the revolution, and consecrated with their blood; it is not obscured by time but shines more luminous in the light of the ages. Wherever the principles they declared have been established, freedom of political and religious thought and action have been enjoyed, and education, enterprise and civilization have advanced. A departure from those principles has entailed oppression, crime and ruin.

"<u>May the Supreme Law-giver of the universe, 'whose service is perfect freedom,' give us the wisdom, fitly and in the spirit of his teachings, to make the laws of this new state forever consecrated as the home of free men...</u>"

"<u>If their affairs are promptly and economically administered, the foundation of good government is secured.</u>" (pp. 95-97, Vol. III, History of Arizona)

John Noble Goodwin (1824-1887), first Territorial Governor
By permission of the Arizona Historical Foundation.

I don't believe that visionary speeches such as these, at such vital junctures of history, are mere words. I am continually impressed by the deep understanding so many 'founding fathers' had of the importance of establishing good foundations for the long term. The pervasive Biblical world view is evident.

Having a sense and understanding of historical destiny is borne out of a Biblical world view. God is the God of history—the unfolding of His creation's story. When we see the world in view of God, we will see God in history. Rather than attributions to chance or other arbitrary views which blind us to historical perspective, we know that here and now each one of us has a place in the intentional history of God.

And, in turn, when men find themselves in an historic moment, I believe they are often moved to see the hand of God, and thus, all the more are moved to call out for His help in awe of Him. The questions that are asked or felt are: 'Why is it that I have been chosen for this historic time?' 'How do I best fulfill this assignment I've been given?'

This awareness seems to be revealed in Governor Goodwin's speech: *"when we consider the importance and grandeur of the work we are selected to perform… to forever shape the destiny of this territory, to lay the foundations of a new state… May the Supreme Law-giver of the universe…give us wisdom."*

In his brief closing speech on the last day of the first Legislative Assembly of the Arizona Territory on November 9, 1864, Governor Goodwin commends the assembly for their great work.

> *"…I have only to express my full appreciation of the diligence and wisdom with which our labors have been prosecuted, and of their great value to the Territory.*
> *"The task before you was indeed one of no ordinary difficulty. Since its acquisition by the United States, the Territory has been almost without law or government. The laws and customs of Spain and Mexico had been clashing with the statute and common law of the United*

States… In addition to the ordinary business of the session, a complete code of laws has been adopted; one which…will compare favorably with the statutes of older States. You have been in session forty-three days, and a greater amount of labor was never performed by a legislative body in the same time.

"I congratulate you on the harmony and good feeling which have characterized your deliberations. At a time when political feelings are strongly excited, you have suffered no party differences to distract your proceedings and divert your attention from the important work before you. You can now separate with the consciousness that your duties are performed." (pp. 127-128, Vol. III, History of Arizona)

THE LOCATION OF THE ARIZONA CAPITOL

After three years in Prescott, the territorial capitol moved to the larger, more established town of Tucson in 1867 until 1877. The Prescottonians, however, wanted it back. After some political battling, the capitol returned to Prescott from 1877 until 1889. Finally, the capitol would move permanently to the more neutral and central site of rapidly growing Phoenix. The original State Capitol building on 17th Avenue and Washington in downtown Phoenix opened in 1900.

The original Capitol is now surrounded by the newer House and Senate buildings just to the east, which opened in 1960, and the Executive Tower directly to the west, which opened in 1974.

During Arizona's colorful territorial days, it carried out its various executive, legislative, and judicial functions while often petitioning for statehood. With the establishment of a permanent and impressive Capitol building, and with a growing population and industry, finally, on June 20, 1910, after nearly 50 years of territorial status, Congress approved the *Enabling Act* to allow New Mexico and Arizona to meet for their respective constitutional conventions for statehood. However, even this did not occur without a fight.

The original Arizona State Capitol in 1909, located in downtown Phoenix – now a museum. By permission of the Arizona State Library, Archives and Public Records

Further understanding concerning the Congressional perspective on the pursuit of statehood is seen in the following article. In response to a request by Arizona Historian George Kelly, the former United States Senator Mark Smith for Arizona wrote a brief summary of the *"Fight for Statehood"* on January 12, 1924, just months before he died. Senator Smith served as a delegate for the Arizona Territory four times from 1887-1895, 1897-1899, 1901-1903, 1905-1909, and then from 1912-1921 as one of the first two U.S. Senators from Arizona. State Historian George Kelly said (*Legislative History of Arizona*, p. 287):

> *"No man in Arizona ever knew more about the statehood fight in Congress than Mark Smith, and no man ever rendered greater service to a constituency than he did in the long struggle."*

Arizona, like most Southern states at the time, was predominantly Democrat in its early days, while the U.S. Congress held a Republican majority. Thus, for many years under the Republicans, there was a move for joint statehood for the two territories of Arizona and New Mexico (under the New Mexico name) so that there would only be one set of new Democrat delegates joining Congress. The vast majority of

Arizonans rejected this idea, having firmly established their own identity and desire for self-governance.

Senator Smith worked year after year to build understanding and a coalition of support within Congress for Arizona's independent statehood. He wrote of the frustrations and some specifics of this battle. One notable incident occurred when Senator Smith thought he had a clear ally across the aisle in Republican Senator James Tawney from Michigan as they approached a pivotal vote. However, at the critical time, Mr. Tawney failed to follow through, and in an apologetic speech acquiesced to his parties' agenda. Senator Smith then writes:

> *"I immediately got the floor and pointing across the aisle at Tawney, who sat near, I said, with the solemn disdain I felt, 'And Joab said to Amasa art thou in health my brother? And took him by the beard with the right hand as to kiss him; but Amasa saw not the sword which was in the left hand of Joab, wherewith he smote him in the fifth rib and spread his bowels out upon the ground.' That was all. The hypocrisy and treachery shown in this short quotation from the Bible brought down such applause from the galleries and from the floor as I had never before heard in that historical hall. The audience had caught the purpose and made instant application. How forceful do we find an apt quotation from Holy Writ. Every paper having a reporter in the press gallery next morning carried in prominent column, praise of the speech and a description of the scene following it."*
>
> *"The recitation of these facts may seem touched with personal egotism to those who never knew me. I disclaim it. My purpose is to record the facts, and my hope is that they will prove to the sons and daughters of my departed friends that I served my country and my state with fidelity, and I want all the people in Arizona to know—what the House and Senate well know—that I saved Arizona from being absorbed and its identity forever lost in the name and destiny of New Mexico."* (p. 294-295, Legislative History of Arizona)

*Marcus Aurelius Smith (1851-1924), first U.S Senator of Arizona
Courtesy of the Library of Congress.*

Once again, we see the impact of Biblical principle effectively changing history, in this case the timely application of scripture from 2 Samuel 20. Senator Smith would go on to play a leading role in building the bi-partisan Congressional support for separate statehood for Arizona during the next few years that would culminate in the *Enabling Act* of June 20, 1910 and prepare the way for the *Arizona Constitutional Convention* in the fall of 1910.

OATHS OF OFFICE – *"SO HELP ME GOD"*

Before we delve into the Constitutional Convention of 1910, I would like to mention two more areas in which God is clearly recognized in Arizona government. First, though easily taken for granted, a very significant government practice is the administration of the Oath of Office. It is not only an important initiation ceremony, but it is a written legal document.

The Oath of Office follows a standard language, which for our purposes, significantly includes the phrases *"I solemnly swear..."* and concludes with *"so help me God."* These oaths are generally administered before witnesses, often including a judge, often in a public ceremony, with the elect placing his hand on a Bible.

This practice is not only reserved for governors and the highest level of officials, but I found in the archives, in both the territorial and early Secretary of State files, numbers of oath documents for a wide range of governmental positions throughout territorial days into statehood. In addition, the administration of the Oath of Office for all judges is required in the Arizona State Constitution—Article 6, Section 26. <u>Therefore, our government practices recognize God, not only in sweeping constitutional statements and proclamations, but also at the individual level in the dedication of government officers</u>.

I found that many oaths of the territorial years had been written out long hand, which does add an even greater sense of personal commitment to the oath. More commonly later on, a standard form was used where blanks were filled in for the office, name, date, etc. Regardless, in every original document I saw, the oath concluded with *"so help me God."* This language was made a part of the written standard during the Civil War, just in time for Arizona's territorial birth and government.

On the subject of the history of the Oath of Office, I recommend an article by Lt. Col. Kenneth Keskel, USAF, entitled: *The Oath of Office – A Historic Guide to Moral Leadership,* <u>Air and Space Power Journal</u>, Winter 2002. In his opening paragraph, he states:

> *"The first law of the United States of America, enacted in the first session of the first Congress on 1 June 1789, was statute 1, chapter 1: an act to regulate the time and manner of administering certain oaths, which established the oath required by civil and military officials to support the Constitution. The founding fathers agreed*

upon the importance of ensuring that officials promised their allegiance; indeed, very little debate occurred before the first Congress passed this statute. Although the wording of the military officer's oath has changed several times in the past two centuries, the basic foundation has withstood the test of time. The current oath is more than a mere formality that adds to the pageantry of a commissioning or promotion ceremony- it provides a foundation for leadership decisions."

Later in the article, Lt. Col. Keskel further states:

*"**So Help Me God**... Controversy over the separation of church and state sometimes clouds this final phrase; nevertheless, it is the most important one in the oath. Our actions have moral and, for those who believe in a Supreme Being, even religious implications... American history is replete with examples of public appeals to a higher being for guidance and protection. The Declaration of Independence includes an appeal "to the Supreme Judge of the world," and, although the Constitution does not include the phrase so help me God in the president's oath, Washington added those words when he took the first oath.*

"The Congressional Record provides superb insight into their meaning: ...For the vast majority of the persons taking the oath, however, this addition will assure a unique degree of personal conviction not otherwise attainable, and will thus prove a welcome source of both personal and national strength.

"So help me God also implies retribution if officers do not keep their word. Compare the part of the Soviet oath that ends with "If I break this solemn vow, may I be severely punished by the Soviet people, universally hated, and despised by the working people." Although that is quite a condemnation, in actuality it is less severe than the potential consequences for someone who has a strong moral or religious foundation. So help me God acknowledges that no stronger commitment exists."

One treasured find at the *Arizona Historical Foundation* at Arizona State University, was President Abraham Lincoln's large (21" x 16") proclamation, accompanied by the seal of the United States and signature of William H. Seward, Secretary of State of the United States, announcing the nomination of John Goodwin as Governor of the Arizona Territory on August 21, 1863. This was issued a few days after the death of the original gubernatorial appointment, John A. Gurley of Ohio. On the back of this proclamation is the handwritten Oath of Office for Governor Goodwin (Goodwin was originally nominated as the Chief Justice for the territory on March 6, 1863):

> *"I, John N. Goodwin, of the State of Maine, having been duly appointed by the President of the United States to be Governor of the Territory of Arizona, do solemnly swear that I have never voluntarily borne arms against the United States since I have been a citizen thereof; that I have voluntarily given no aid, countenance, counsel or encouragement to persons engaged in armed hostility thereto; that I have neither sought nor accepted nor attempted to exercise the functions of any office whatever under any authority or pretended authority in hostility to the United States; that I have not yielded a voluntary support to any pretended government, authority, power or constitution within the United States, hostile or inimical thereto. And I do further swear that, to the best of my knowledge and ability, I will support and defend the constitution of the United States against all enemies, foreign and domestic; that I will bear true faith and allegiance to the same; that I take this obligation freely, without any mental reservation or purpose of evasion, and that I will well and faithfully discharge the duties of the office on which I am about to enter: <u>So help me God</u>."*

PROCLAMATIONS OF THANKSGIVING DAY

As I was searching through various boxes and folders in the archives at the State Capitol for original Oaths of Office, I began to find among these several "Proclamations of Thanksgiving." It became evident that there was an annual practice in territorial days for a statewide proclamation for a day of thanksgiving to God for our blessings received during the year corresponding to the national Presidential 'Thanksgiving' proclamations issued every November.

Earlier, I presented President Abraham Lincoln's proclamation of a day of "humiliation, fasting and prayer" (p. 37). In similar unabashed language acknowledging God, these Thanksgiving Day proclamations were issued in Arizona. Of those I stumbled upon, my favorites are from 1893 and 1894, complete with their gold-gilded Arizona territorial Seals affixed.

Here is the transcription of the 1894 Thanksgiving Proclamation in its entirety issued by territorial Governor Louis Hughes:

Thanksgiving Proclamation.
Territory of Arizona.
Executive Department.

Phoenix, Sunday, November 11, 1894.

To the People of the Territory of Arizona, Greeting:

Recognizing the manifold blessings of a kind Providence during the past year, and in accordance with a revered custom of the American people, and in conformity with the proclamation of the President of the United States, I do hereby appoint Thursday, November 29, 1894, a day of Thanksgiving and Prayer to be observed by the people throughout the Territory.
Truly the hearts of patriots ought to be filled with gratitude and thanksgiving when we consider the outcome of the threatening events of the past year, which demonstrate that the principles of our government when in the keeping of wise and courageous hands are sufficient to meet and overcome the greatest danger which may menace the integrity or perpetuity of the Republic.
Since the people of our Territory have been especially favored with more than ordinary peace, plenty

and prosperity, and the absence of want and distress in its many forms, let us with grateful hearts cease from all business pursuits on that day and with one accord "Give thanks unto the Lord for His merciful kindness to the children of all men."

In Testimony *I have hereunto set my hand and caused to be affixed the Great Seal of the Territory.*

Done at Phoenix, the Capital, the Eleventh day of November, in the year of our Lord, One Thousand Eight Hundred and Ninety-four, and of our American Independence the One Hundred and Eighteenth.

Louis C. Hughes,

By the Governor:
Charles M. Bruce,
Secretary of the Territory.

I give here a brief biography of the issuer of this 1894 *Thanksgiving Proclamation*, Territorial Governor Louis C. Hughes, who in the words of at least one biographer, *"was one of the few governors who helped clean up Arizona and prepare it for statehood."* (http://jeff.scott.tripod.com/Hughes.html)

Louis Cameron Hughes (1842-1915) served in his capacity as territorial governor of Arizona from 1893 to 1896. He was considered a *"highly principled reformer."* He endorsed women's suffrage, cleaning up the election process, prohibition, and enforcement of laws preserving the Sabbath and prohibiting prostitution and adultery.

He grew up as an orphan in Pennsylvania and served as an 'indentured servant' to a farmer until he was 16 years of age. As an abolitionist from the earliest age, he enlisted in the Union army at the outbreak of the Civil War. Following the war, he attended a seminary and then continued on in higher education. Later, as a lawyer, he came to Arizona with his wife Josephine in

1871, where he practiced law before the Arizona Territorial Supreme Court.

Governor Louis C. Hughes (1842-1915), c.1890
By permission of the Arizona State Archives and Library

He was a city councilman for Tucson, and Attorney General of the Arizona Territory. He started the *Daily Bulletin* in 1877, which became the *Arizona Star*, which continues in operation to this day. He was even known to preach on street corners in Tucson as a member of the Salvation Army. He continually promoted such causes as temperance, women's suffrage, and Arizona statehood.

Governor George Hunt referred to his wife, Josephine Hughes, as the "Mother of Arizona." She was a member of the Women's Suffrage Movement, and a friend of Frances Williard and Susan

B. Anthony. She was instrumental in the establishment of the Women's Christian Temperance Union of Arizona.

As to the *Thanksgiving Proclamation* itself, I would like to emphasize a few of its most striking points. First, the body of the proclamation begins and ends by acknowledging God:

> *"Recognizing the manifold blessings of a kind Providence..."*

> *"...with one accord "Give thanks unto the Lord for His merciful kindness to the children of all men.""*

It affirms the link with our nation and our Christian heritage, since the very custom of Thanksgiving Day was borne through the Christian Pilgrims:

> *"in accordance with a revered custom of the American people, and in conformity with the proclamation of the President of the United States..."*

It asserts the value of good government and governmental officials:

> *"that the principles of government when in the keeping of wise and courageous hands are sufficient to meet and overcome the greatest danger which may menace the integrity or perpetuity of the Republic."*

I found the original document, complete with its golden Arizona State Seal, to be beautiful in both content and form.

This document did not stand alone, either, as I happened on four or five other similar proclamations in archival boxes, dated both before and after this 1894 proclamation. I believe it would be worthwhile to pursue a more in-depth search and review of all of the *Thanksgiving Proclamations* issued by our Arizona government.

Following is an image of the original 1894 *Thanksgiving Proclamation:*

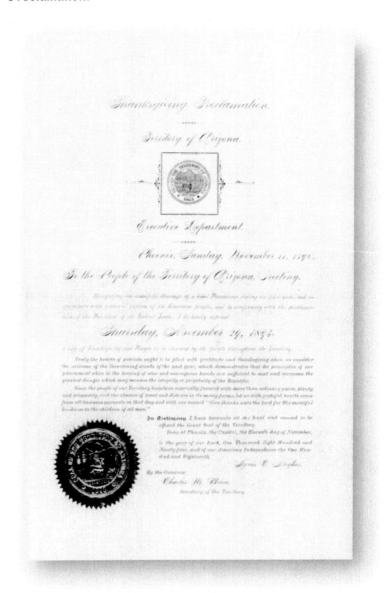

The 1894 Arizona Thanksgiving Proclamation
Courtesy of the Arizona State Library, Archives and Public Records

*Enlarged inset:
Chaplain Seaborn Crutchfield,
age 73 at the time of this photo
among members of the 1910
Constitutional Convention*

*Members of the Arizona Constitutional Convention of 1910
By permission of the Arizona State Library, Archives and Public Records*

VI. The Arizona Constitutional Convention of 1910 and Chaplain Seaborn Crutchfield

"The first order of business, '(a) Prayer by the Chaplain'"
– The Records of the Arizona Constitutional Convention of 1910

We now turn our attention to the *Arizona Constitutional Convention of 1910*. Arizona had finally been granted its petition to form a constitution for statehood. The convention was convened beginning at Noon on October 10, 1910 on the third floor House Chamber at the original State Capitol building at 1700 W. Washington in downtown Phoenix. It was set to stay in session until completion on December 9, 1910. Fifty-two delegates representing regions throughout Arizona were elected on September 12, 1910 to form the convention body for the purpose of drafting the proposed state constitution.

"The Records of the Arizona Constitutional Convention of 1910" (from here on referred to as ***RACC***), edited by John S. Goff, 1991, provide the most accessible historical record for the proceedings. On the third day of the Convention, the business of Mr. J. A. Larrabee of Tucson was approved as the official stenographer for recording all of the proceedings [p. 23, ***RACC***]. On the fifth day of the convention the "standing rules" by the special Committee on Rules and Order of Business of the convention were adopted, which included as the first order of business, "(a) Prayer by the Chaplain" [p. 26, ***RACC***].

During the second week of the convention there was a lapse in the verbatim record of the proceedings when, for two days, they used only a legal minutes format rather than verbatim journaling. For these two days, only a brief report of the type of actions was recorded, eliminating the speeches and discussions, which also eliminated the recording of the chaplain's prayers. Thus, all we have is the notation, "chaplain prayer" for these two days. However, after discussion on the floor of the convention, the detailed verbatim procedure was reinstituted for the remainder of the sessions.

Even so, I still find it remarkable and, I suspect, highly unusual that the legal record would include the chaplain prayers verbatim. This practice may also have made the prayers more accessible to the media and for publication. <u>At least one prayer is even purported to have influenced the decision by President Taft to sign Arizona into statehood without further delay</u>.

The Constitutional Convention prayers of Chaplain Seaborn Crutchfield were given immediately after roll call at the beginning of each day of the session. In all, about 50 prayers are recorded verbatim, all of which are compiled in the following chapter. But first, I will provide his brief biography.

Seaborn Crutchfield was born March 15, 1837, near Monticello in Wayne County, Kentucky. The *Arizona Republican* and *Phoenix Gazette* conducted interviews with him in his latter years which provided some interesting biographical information just a few months before his death on June 26, 1927.

The chaplain was named for his grandfather, who was born at sea while his grandfather's parents emigrated from Denmark. [His grandfather became a pioneer Methodist preacher in Kentucky who would establish a church that still stands. He was also a co-laborer with the famous Methodist Circuit Riding Revivalist Peter Cartwright (1785-1872).]

Though Kentucky was a neutral state in the Civil War, young Seaborn, at age 24, was not neutral and joined the South, eventually joining up with John Morgan's Raiders in 1861. After participating in daring raids into Indiana and Ohio, their band was cut off and nearly wiped out. Seaborn managed to escape and lead a small remnant back toward and within sight of his Kentucky home and safety, but he took five bullets and was captured and imprisoned in Ohio for more than a year until the end of the war. As he said, *"It was hard. But it was the war."*

"The North was wrong, the South was wrong; Lincoln was right and again he was wrong. It was all a peculiar muddle, but perhaps it's worked out for the best. Yes—for the best. Certainly! For slavery was wrong. No man has a right to possess another man's soul, and his body. I say that—having owned slaves. They took mine away. And the cost was mighty heavy. But I'm glad they did. I disagree with the way they did it. Gradual emancipation was the better course it seemed then, as it seems today. But Lincoln was a wonderful man, it's easy to see now that the powder and the smoke—and Lincoln himself—are gone." – Reverend Seaborn Crutchfield, March 14, 1927

In 1868, Crutchfield went west to Texas and soon entered the ministry after perhaps serving some time as a sheriff. He was married in 1869 to Miss Ellen Harris and they had two sons and two daughters. He traveled thousands of miles and raised a family as a preacher under the North Texas Conference of the Methodist Episcopal Church for nearly 40 years until his retirement with them. During this time, he put all of his children through higher education. His two sons would also become Methodist ministers, as well as one of his sons-in-law. His wife Ellen is reported to have died in 1907, which may have precipitated his move to Arizona. He may also have gone to California for some time before coming to Arizona (his daughter lived there).

In 1908 he established a small church in a little adobe building in the village of Safford. He was pleased to report, nearly twenty years later, that the church had grown substantially and was thriving. His son James was elected a Maricopa County delegate for the Constitutional Convention of 1910. I can only guess it was through his son's connections that Crutchfield was offered the opportunity to serve as chaplain.

In 1910 Crutchfield married Miss Lillian Caldwell, who died in 1918. In 1920, he married Miss Esther Schroll at Newport, Kentucky, which evidently was a marriage that had its trials (note the comments in the will below). He lived his last years at his home near the corner of 11th Avenue and Madison in downtown Phoenix, less than a mile from the State Capitol.

The following is a transcription from a document reputed to have been prepared on Seaborn Crutchfield's personal stationary (I don't know if the typos are his or copy errors):

House of Representatives, State of Arizona, Fifth Legislature

I, Seaborn Crutchfield.
Not unmindful of the uncertainty of life and the certaincy of death in the event I should die "unexpectedly" intestate and inasmuch as I made a "will" at Ada Oklahoma nearly two years ago my son Wallace M. Crutchfield's name was signed to that "Will" as a witness and inasmuch as that "Will" has been mislaid "destroyed or stolen" I make this in lieu of that "Will" And inasmuch as Esther Schroll has come into my life and home I make this change in my "Will" in the event that that "Will" should be discovered after my death.
First: I make my son Wallace M. Crutchfield the executor of my estate without bond.
Second: At this date I own no man one single dollar nor am I security for any man for one single dollar and I own a house and lot and a small tenant house and garage on the corner of 11th Avenue and Madison street in the the City of Phoenix Arizona valued at about $4500.00. and automobile valued at about 400.00. a note on my son James Crutchfield for about $825.00. ballance ona note on J.I. Ferguson for $250.00. have two checks on the State Treasurer for $55.00. deposited in the Valley Bank $351.50. and my wife owes me $125.00. for loaned money to buy a Piana aggregating $6336.50.
Third: In the event I should die unexpectedly my son Wallace shall dispose of my effects as follows = He shall have $150.00. for his travelling expenses as he lives in Hugo Oklahoma' My daughter Josephene has had the equivalent of $200.00. in an Automobile transaction and

my daughter Lura shall have $200.00. my son James shall have $200.00 and my son Wallace shall have $200.00 and the rest of my estate shall be equally divided with the five legatees Viz. Josephine, James, Wallace, Lura and Esther my wife provided she does not leave my home or enter legal proceedings against me (as she is constantly threatening to do) in which event she shall have only $100.00 and that will buy her a Rail Road ticket back to her people in Newport Kentucky.
    In witness whereof I have signed this "Will"
Seaborn Crutchfield
Made 1921 Signed April 7th 1925
Witness.....
Laura E. Davis, Adam A Nober, Apr 1st 1925

Interesting to note, Crutchfield was an unswerving and outspoken life-long Democrat since the earliest age he could vote. Today, most ministers are expected to veil their political views, especially in public. Not so from our nation's founding until the relatively recent past.

"I voted for a Democrat at my first election and I shall vote the Democratic ticket till I die... A Democrat yesterday, today and on..." (from an interview, Arizona Republican, March 14, 1927)

After the Constitutional Convention, the chaplain served in every Arizona legislative session, except one, until his death at age 90 in 1927. Following is an excerpt from the *Citizen Capital Bureau* of January, 25, 1921, which said of Crutchfield, who was then 83:

    "One of the most picturesque figures of the fifth legislature is the Reverend Crutchfield, chaplain of the lower house. The chaplain of the house takes more than a passing interest in legislative affairs. All through the sessions he may be seen attentively following every move and motion. With a shocked head of gray cocked to one side, with a hand to his ear, he listens to every word

uttered as though summing things up as material for his divine supplications.

"The Reverend Crutchfield belongs to the old school of preachers, the kind who speak from the heart. There is nothing formal or bookish about his prayers. On the contrary they are original from beginning to end, and are carefully followed as a result...

"The other day the newspaper reporters were not unpleasantly shocked by hearing the chaplain offer up prayers for themselves. In the memory of many present it was the first time that any divine had been so thoughtful as to offer a special prayer for the reporters. He prayed that they would refrain from writing sensational headlines or writing anything at variance with the truth—anything that might bring into disrepute the fairest city west of the Rockies...

"Reverend Crutchfield's prayers are well received, and are generally regarded as a refreshing change from the ordinary prayers which one sometimes hears in legislative halls. They are pointed and outspoken and carry a tone of sincerity which makes every listener willing to tackle the duties of the day with zest and earnestness."

In fact, the ultimate responsibility he felt toward his chaplaincy is evident in the following account given by the *Arizona Republican* in the article reporting his death on June 27, 1927:

"It was April 20, the day the Eighth Legislature adjourned sine die... that Rev. Crutchfield sustained the injury which it is believed hastened, if not caused the end, and cut short his life's ambition to live to the century milestone.

The aged minister was in the act of getting into his automobile in front of his home, 1018 West Madison street, to go to the state capitol shortly before 10 o'clock, April 20, to deliver the invocation incident to the opening of the morning session of the lower house, when his foot

> *slipped from the running board and he fell heavily to the ground.*
>
> *His grandson, who was waiting to drive him to the capitol, assisted Rev. Crutchfield to his feet, and Mrs. Crutchfield, who witnessed the accident, insisted that the minister return to the house, fearing he had injured himself. Rev. Crutchfield, however, refused to hear the plea and went on to the capitol with his grandson.*
>
> *After being helped from the car in front of the entrance to the building, Rev. Crutchfield declared he could not go farther and asked that a substitute chaplain be called. He refused to budge from a bench in front of the building until the substitute arrived, although Mrs. Crutchfield, who had been called, insisted he return home.*
>
> *While sitting on the bench, numerous of the chaplain's friends came by and greeted him. To none of them did he mention the accident, but met each with his usual cheery greeting and friendly words. When he was removed to his home, several minutes later, and two physicians had examined him, it was found that he had sustained a broken right hip joint. For a time, it was feared that the injury would cause his death within a few hours, but the rugged, determined spirit of the aged minister and his hard constitution won out..."*

During his chaplaincy, he established a good friendship with Governor Hunt, and was asked by the governor to provide the invocation at each of his inauguration ceremonies. These prayers became famous, at least in part, for the phrase he included in each—asking *"the Divine blessing upon the 'mugwamp' Democrats and the disgruntled Republicans."*

From *George W. P. Hunt and His Arizona* by John S. Goff (p.145-146):

> *"On New Year's Day 1923, George W. P. Hunt again became governor of Arizona... The governor-elect had planned no ceremony but would instead simply take his oath in the governor's office. However the Chief Justice*

of the state decided it would be better to have the swearing-in ceremonies in the House chamber since so many had arrived to witness the event. Even then Hunt complained that the room was "crowded to suffocation." The highlight of the proceedings was the invocation offered by the Reverend Seaborn Crutchfield, the aged clergyman who had been chaplain of the Constitutional Convention of 1910, and who now served in like capacity in the Arizona House of Representatives. Crutchfield began, "O Thou Eternal Jehovah this inaugural day as this grand Old Roman assumes the gubernatorial responsibility of this great commonwealth we stand as hopeful, happy expectants of better days for Arizona," but as he warmed to his subject his partisan political feelings began to show more and more. Among other things he asked for protection of Hunt in that "During his tenure of office spare him the unjust, unreasonable criticism of disgruntled, mugwamp Democrats, shrewd and designing Republican politicians and sensational headlines of newspapers."

Then two years later at Hunt's next inauguration (p. 162):

"On January 5, 1925, Hunt became in the words of the press, "George the Fifth." Chief Justice McAllister administered the oath of office but once again the star of the ceremonies was the aged Reverend Crutchfield who asked Divine protection for "this grand Old Roman," and specifically once more asked for the help of the Lord in the Governor's dealings with disloyal Democrats, and "shrewd designing Republican politicians," as well as protection against sensational newspaper headlines."

In another article that honors his 86th birthday in 1923, it was said:

"Mr. Crutchfield has a longer record of chaplaincy, perhaps, than any other minister in this country and is probably better known as a chaplain than any other

except the Rev. Henry Cowden, for so long chaplain of the house of representatives of the national legislature."

These are rather high accolades for one whose career in chaplaincy did not begin until age 73 after he had retired from a nearly 40-year pastoral career! It reveals the enduring force of character he displayed among his peers during the formation of our state.

When I was first introduced to a few of the Crutchfield prayers in the legislative record, I knew nothing of the man behind them. It is clear that Reverend Crutchfield, with all of his colorful personal history, was used by God to help establish good foundations in the government of Arizona. His life itself spans and seems to capture the historical era of our nation in great civil turmoil during the birth of the state of Arizona.

Having given this brief summary of his life as discovered through limited historical records, I now turn to the introduction of his prayers given at the *Arizona Constitutional Convention of 1910.*

Nearly every prayer of the Constitutional Convention was recorded verbatim. There are occasional typing, punctuation and capitalization inconsistencies, perhaps largely due to variations in the different stenographers' styles and capabilities.

For the sake of my own accuracy, and in the spirit of my own version of legislative protocol, I have undergone three 'readings' of each prayer. The 'first reading' was to type in each prayer. The 'second reading' is re-reading it against the original record. For the 'third reading' I have re-read them again and given each a brief title heading. I have only corrected the occasional obvious typos, such as "Theee", without attempting to address any grammatical issues. I do not know if the original stenographers were given written prayers to copy or if it was all taken by dictation, though I believe it was the latter.

I think you will find that the content of Chaplain Crutchfield's prayers supersede any inconsistencies in grammar and language.

Mulford Winsor, Constitutional Convention delegate from Yuma who later served as Arizona State Historian, is quoted in the Arizona Capitol museum on the 3rd floor:

> *"Seaborn Crutchfield, a former Texas sheriff, later a circuit-riding preacher, and above all a fine, sturdy, sincere character... the prayers he addressed to the Throne of Grace, if not models of diction, were classics of frankness."*

Chaplain Seaborn Crutchfield (1837-1927), at age 88 in 1925
By permission of the Arizona State Library, Archives and Public Records

VII. The Prayers of Chaplain Seaborn Crutchfield

"The effective, fervent prayer of a righteous man avails much."
– James 5:16

Here is the prayer by the Chaplain at the conclusion of the convention, which gained national attention and was said to actually influence President Taft in signing Arizona into statehood:

> *"Oh Lord, I certainly hope that President Taft will not turn down the Constitution, as some say he will, for a little thing like the initiative and referendum. That would be pretty small. I can tell you, Lord, you'll be doing the people of Arizona a big favor if You will influence the President of the United States to let us have a government of our own. Don't let him be so narrow and partisan as to refuse us self-government, under a constitution like we want."*

It has been my pleasure to find this buried treasure within the legal record of the Constitutional Convention of 1910. They are of a notable humble and prophetic character, to go with their boldness. I have set them in chronological order, providing the day and date they occurred, and page number they appear in ***The Records of the Arizona Constitutional Convention of 1910***, edited by John S. Goff, which I refer to as ***RACC***.

I have provided a single full page for each day's prayer. By my count there were 54 total prayers given at the convention, including three that were not recorded verbatim and one recitation of the "Lord's Prayer" by his son, James Crutchfield.

On a few occasions I include additional legislative record as appropriate. I have entitled each prayer and provided a Table of Contents for easier reference. Some of you may wish to take advantage of this format to use them in part or whole as model prayers to re-connect with the vein of history of our Arizona government. Many are as relevant and effectual today as they were nearly one hundred years ago.

Along with creating titles to distinguish each prayer, I have tried to underline some of the prophetic declarations and striking themes evident in the body of the prayers. The reader may wish to highlight additional themes and phrases that stand out.

For those of you not wishing to read through all of the Crutchfield prayers at this time, you may choose to skim through them and then move on to further discussions of the documentary history of God in Arizona government, which I continue in the next chapter on page 138. I cover our State Constitution's Preamble, Seal and Motto, and other developments toward statehood in chapters VIII, IX, and X, with final conclusions in chapter XI.

Table of Contents for Chaplain Crutchfield Prayers

#1:	Wisdom of Solomon and Godly Guidance	84
#2:	Brightest Star in the Union	85
#3:	We Seek Thine Aid and Blessings First	86
#4:	Let Love and Peace Abound	87
#5:	We Dedicate Ourselves unto Thee	88
#6:	Our Hearts are Filled with Gratitude	89
#7:	Help Us Become a Great and Good People	90
•	A place for your own prayer for good government	91
•	A place for your own prayer for good government	92
#8:	Thy Spirit to Abide With Us	93
#9:	Replace Evil with Good	94
#10:	Lead Us in the Paths of a Righteous and Holy Life	95
#11:	We Can All Approach the Throne of Grace	96
#12:	Pour Forth Thy Spirit upon Our Heads	97
#13:	Building the Foundations	98
#14:	Lead Us in the Straight and Narrow Pathways	99
#15:	No Petty Petitions or Measures Incorporated	100
#16:	Bless These Men with Wisdom and Knowledge	101
#17:	We Thank Thee that We are Still Alive	102
#18:	We Acknowledge Thee as Our God and Leader	103
#19:	May There Be No Acrimony, Bickering or Strife	104
#20:	How Excellent is Thy Name in All the Earth	105
#21:	May None Throw a Bomb in Our State	106
#22:	Surrounded By So Many Circumstances of Mercy	107
#23:	All-Wise Heavenly Father	108
#24:	We Acknowledge Thy Divinity and Mightiness	109
#25:	May We Begin Right, Continue Right, and End Right	110
#26:	Stand on Record as Perpetuating Good Government	111
•	James Crutchfield Leads the Lord's Prayer	112
#27:	Oh Lord, Meet with Us Today	113
#28:	May Our Thoughts Be Acceptable in Thy Sight	114
#29:	Our Help Cometh from God	115
#30:	Showers from Heaven	116
#31:	The Rights of None Be Forgotten	117
#32:	O Lord, Give Audience Now as We Pray	118
#33:	Great Cause of Liberty at Heart	119
#34:	The Desert Shall Blossom as the Rose	120
#35:	Nothing but the Glory of God	121
#36:	Very Keen Sense of Our Unworthiness	122
#37:	Thanksgiving Day	123
#38:	We Need Thee Every Hour	124

#39:	Keep the Love of Freedom Ever Alive in Our Hearts	125
#40:	Public Sentiment Will Ultimately Be Adjusted	126
#41:	Thank You for the Privilege of Worshipping You	127
•	A place for your own prayer for good government	128
#42:	Wisdom Even to the End of This Great Labor	129
#43:	Forgive Us, O Lord, For Our Sins	130
#44:	May Arizona Become One of the Fairest States	131
#45:	We Dare Not Take One Step without Thy Aid	132
#46:	Now Help Us to Pray	133
#47:	Take All Our Sins Away	134
#48:	That We Shall Have a Clean and Good Constitution	135
#49:	All Sing "America", Approval of God and Men	136
#50:	Dismiss Us, Lord, With Thy Blessing	137

A NOTE TO INTERCESSORS:

Proverbs 11:11 says...
> *"By the blessing of the upright the city is exalted, but it is overthrown by the mouth of the wicked."*

Romans 12:14 says...
> *"Bless those who persecute you; bless and do not curse."*

In light of the admonition to pray *"first of all for all authorities..."* from 1 Timothy 2:1-4, the verses above make clear that we are to **bless** our government leaders regardless of their character or stance on social and political issues. This does not mean that we turn a blind eye, but in the midst of what we may see, all the more ask for God to reveal Himself to those for whom we pray, and to grant them wisdom and protection. Though, at times, we may be particularly tested in governmental prayer, if we humble ourselves and abide in God's love, *our* hearts *will* be changed and we will become more effective and see God work through our prayers for better government.

> *"Love suffers long and is kind...does not seek its own, is not provoked...does not rejoice in iniquity, but rejoices in the truth; bears all things... And now abide in faith, hope, love, these three; but the greatest of these is love."*
> *– 1 Corinthians 13:4-7, 13*

#1: *Wisdom of Solomon and Godly Guidance*

Monday morning, October 10, 1910 [p. 1, ***RACC***]:

[Words missing but *Arizona Republican*, (Phoenix), October 11, 1910, reported it included:]

"'As King Solomon prayed for guidance to wisely rule a great people, so we ask Thee to direct us in the adoption of a wise and just constitution.' Also included was the Lord's Prayer. The portion which the *Arizona Gazette*, October 10, 1910, reported was: "Thank God for the circumstances surrounding us today. We pray for guidance that our hearts, hand and tongues may glorify Thy name. We thank Thee for this grand body of sedate men. We trust they are patriots and believe they will frame such a constitution as will bless the teeming thousands that will flow into the state in coming years. We pray for divine guidance for the man who will have the gavel in his hands during this convention.""

#2: Brightest Star in the Union

Tuesday morning, October 11, 1910 [p. 9, ***RACC***]:

Mr. President: Convention will come to order.
The secretary will call the roll. Quorum present.
Mr. President: Gentlemen of the convention, will you please rise, and Reverend Seaborn Crutchfield will pronounce the invocation.

Reverend Crutchfield: "Oh, Lord! We come before Thee, the members of this convention, in the attitude of prayer, and we ask Thy blessings upon each and every member of this convention. <u>Inspire their minds with the love of their state and the love of their country that they may be guided this day by Thy Holy Spirit</u>. Be mindful for each member of this convention that he may have prudence that he may have only the desire to serve his people in this convention. We pray the blessings upon the President that he may be guided by the Holy Spirit and be granted wisdom as the leading officer of the convention. <u>We pray Thee, Oh Lord, that this body of men, the representatives of the people of Arizona, may frame such a constitution as will meet the approval of every citizen and that it may grant unto Arizona statehood, and place it among the grand galaxy of states in these United States, and that Arizona may be the brightest star in the Union</u>. Grant us peace and love of country and love of mankind in our hearts and guide us through this day of work. These blessings we would ask of Thee, in the name of Jesus Christ, Thy Son. Amen."

#3: *We Seek Thine Aid and Blessings First*

Wednesday morning, October 12, 1910 [p. 13, ***RACC***]:

"Kind and heavenly Father, we are truly thankful that not one of these men are ill or any accident has happened to them; that they have been permitted to come to the chamber this morning in health and peace prepared for the great duties of another day in the Constitutional Convention. Oh Lord, it has been said that we should not attempt the work until we have sought Thine aid and Thy Blessings. We do invoke Thy mercies and blessings upon the members of this Convention, that they may be guided in all the work which they undertake this day. <u>Bless each and every member that he may be inspired with a love of the labor and of the people which he represents, and now, Oh Lord, help us and help the members of this convention to so live, and act that they may be worthy of Thy choicest blessings and all of this we ask in the name of Jesus Christ, Thy Son. Amen.</u>"

#4: *Let Love and Peace Abound*

Thursday morning, October 13, 1910 [p. 21, ***RACC***]:

"Kind and Merciful Heavenly Father, our God, again we come before Thee to ask Thy blessings upon this convention. We thank Thee that they have been permitted to meet again in health and in peace and we ask Thee to pronounce a blessing upon their heads this day. Bless the leading officer with wisdom and understanding of his duties that he may guide the work in a prudent and judicious manner. And now, Oh Lord, there are likely to be contentions and disagreeances [sic] arise among the members will Thou temper the minds of these men to wisdom and grant that they may be guided in all their words and acts both in convention matters and in their acts to each other. <u>Let love and peace abound in all hearts and charity abide there too</u>. Forgive us of our sins and remember us in all the ways of life and save us in Thy Kingdom is the supplication of all our hearts today, and these blessings we ask of Thee in the name of Thine only Begotten Son, Amen."

#5: *We Dedicate Ourselves unto Thee*

Friday morning, October 14, 1910 [p. 24, ***RACC***]:

"Our Great and merciful heavenly Father, we again present ourselves before Thee in Constitutional Convention assembled, and before taking up the duties of the convention would ask of Thee a blessing. Oh Lord hear our petition this day. We ask Thee for wisdom and prudence in all works and measures that may come before the convention this day. <u>Help us to be good men and great men, and bless us with that love and charity for each other that we may say and do good things to each other</u>, and cause that no strife or contentions may arise among these men to hinder them in the great work which is to [be] perform[ed.] Bless the absent families of these men and comfort and cheer their hearts and grant them your protection. Now, <u>Oh Lord we dedicate ourselves unto Thee for we know that Thou art all merciful and Thou are all love</u>. Forgive us of our sins and save us in Thy kingdom is our supplication and our prayer, all blessings we ask Thee in the name of the Redeemer, ever so Amen."

#6: *Our Hearts are Filled with Gratitude*

Saturday morning, October 15, 1910 [p. 36, ***RACC***]:

"Kind and Gracious God, the Father of the Universe, we again come before Thee invoking Thy Holy Spirit upon us for another day of work in this convention and before we commence the labors of the day we desire to call upon Thy mercies for a blessing and the guidance of our every thought and action this day. We realize that we are weak and sinful in many of our ways and we desire to become righteous and that it is through Thy grace that we are permitted to meet again[;] therefore we approach Thy Throne of Grace in humility asking Thy forgiveness and Thine approval and with hearts filled with gratitude for all Thy blessing we do beseech Thee to continue the Blessings unto us. <u>Bless these men with wisdom and prudence, and with a knowledge of the great work of constitution building, that whatever they may do, or say, or measures they may submit, that these measures will be acts of prudence and wisdom, having the love of liberty in their hearts, when they adopt them into the Constitution of the State</u>. Be mindful of us Oh Lord in all that Thou seest that we need, and accept the privilege of meeting together again in peace for the labors of the Convention. All blessings we ask of Thee through the worthy name of Thine only Begotten Son. Amen."

#7: *Help Us Become a Great and Good People*

Monday morning, October 17, 1910 [p. 42-43, ***RACC***]:

"Our Lord and God, we would call upon Thee again to ask of Thee a blessing upon this another new day and another week. <u>Before we begin the task of this day we desire to petition Thee for Thy Spirit that whatsoever these men may undertake they may be guided by inspiration. Now O Lord we do not want to undertake this great work without Thy Holy Spirit being poured upon us</u>[;] therefore we ask that we have it for guidance in all the labors of this day. There may be complications arise and discussions arise which may perplex the minds of these men, now heavenly Father we ask Thee to grant them wisdom and prudence to solve all such complications. Bless the president of this convention and to preside over these meetings and bless also the members and especially the chairmen of the committees that their duties may be performed without friction or complications or if there are any that they may have the wisdom in solving them. <u>Bless all Thy people of this State and this great nation and all those who have duties of office to perform. Help us O Lord to become a great and good people</u>, and we all hail in the Prayer of Thine only begotten Son, "Our Father who are in heaven hallowed be Thy name. Thy Kingdom come, Thy will be done on earth as it is in heaven, and give us this day our daily bread and forgive us our trespasses as we forgive those who trespass against us. Suffer us not to be led into temptation but deliver us from evil for Thine is the kingdom and the Power and the Glory, forever, Amen.""

You May Write Your Own Prayer Here…

Tuesday morning, October 18, 1910 [p. 49, ***RACC***]:

"Prayer by chaplain." *[only entry]*

Write your own prayer for good government for the leaders and state of Arizona here:

You May Write Your Own Prayer Here...

Wednesday morning, October 19, 1910 [p. 52, ***RACC***]:

"Prayer by chaplain." *[only entry]*

*Note: On p. 54, ***RACC*** it was determined that the stenographers return to the more detailed journaling of the daily proceedings rather than use the abbreviated form of these last two days.

Write your own prayer for good government for the leaders and state of Arizona here:

#8: *Thy Spirit to Abide With Us*

Thursday morning, October 20, 1910 [p. 56-57, ***RACC***]:

"Almighty God, our Heavenly Father, we thank Thee for bringing us safely to this place, and we call upon our God for His blessings on this beautiful day. We thank Thee for the happy lives that Thou hast given us, and that we have been spared another day to undertake the duties assigned us. We ask that we may have Thy Spirit to abide with us, and attend us in all that we may have to undertake, and that there may not one step be taken that would not be for the best good of the people. We realize, Oh God, our weakness, and that we are considerably led into paths of temptation, and that we need Thy Holy Spirit as a guidance in all the walks of life. Deliver our minds from every evil thought and replace the evil with good. <u>Cause that all the acts of these men may be for the good of this great country and for the good of the State</u>. Bless the president of this convention that he may have an abundance of Thy Spirit to guide him in his many duties as the leader of these men and bless every member of this convention. Oh, Lord, we would dedicate ourselves, and all that we do unto Thee, knowing that Thou art all wise and Almighty. All these blessings, we ask in the name of Thine only Begotten Son, Jesus Christ our Redeemer, Amen."

#9: *Replace Evil with Good*

Friday morning, October 21, 1910 [p. 65, ***RACC***]:

"Oh Lord, our Heavenly Father, we thank Thee that we have been preserved on this another beautiful day and we call upon our God for His blessings on this day. We thank Thee that we are happy and healthy and that our lives have been spared and that we are permitted to meet for the duties of another day. We ask that we may have Thy Spirit to abide with us and attend us in all that we may have to undertake and that there may not one step be taken that would not be for the best good of the people. <u>We realize that we are weak and that we are led into paths of temptation and that we need Thy Holy Spirit as a guidance in all walks of life. Deliver our minds from every evil thought and replace the evil with good</u>. Cause that all the acts of these men may be for the good of this great country and for the good of the State. Bless the president of this convention that he may have an abundance of Thy Spirit to guide him in his many duties as the leader of these men and bless every member in his efforts to keep his pledges and to perform the work that he has been elected to do. Now <u>Oh, Lord, we would dedicate ourselves and all that we do unto Thee, knowing that Thou art all wise and Thou art merciful, and will bless our petitions in as much as they seem unto You as our needs. All these blessings we ask of Thee in the name of Thine only Begotten Son, Jesus Christ our Redeemer, Amen.</u>"

#10: *Lead Us in the Paths of a Righteous and Holy Life*

Saturday morning, October 22, 1910 [p. 69, ***RACC***]:

"Oh Lord and Gracious Heavenly Father, we thank Thee that we have been permitted to rise from our rest to life again and enjoy the blessing of health, and for these blessings we feel very grateful in our hearts. We pray that we may have guidance this day, and <u>we would not have Thee take Thine hand from us, but we would [pray] that Thou should lead us in the paths of righteous and Holy life</u>. These men need Thy blessings and guidance in the work they have before them, and we thank Thee that none of them have been sick or none of them called home to their families who might be ill, for Thou hast blessed them and their families with health, and privileged them to meet again on this day the last day of a week of diligent service, and Thy blessings have attended them in another week's labor. <u>Now Oh Lord, we pray Thee that Thou will continue Thy blessings and Thy mercies and all these we ask Thee in the name of Thy Son Jesus Christ, our Redeemer, Amen</u>."

#11: We Can All Approach the Throne of Grace

Monday morning, October 24, 1910 [p. 71-72, ***RACC***]:

"Almighty God our Heavenly Father we thank Thee for the past Sabbath day for which we have had relaxation from the busy bustle of the past week and that we are permitted to come back here refreshed in mind and body for work. We pray Thee that we may have the guidance of Thy Holy Spirit in all we do. Some of the pages may not have had the opportunity of worship yesterday. Some of these men may not have the opportunity of going to their respective places of worship, but make our prayers responsive to the will of the Lord so we may accomplish that which we are sent into the world to do. <u>We can all both Jew and Greek and Gentile, bond and free approach the Throne of Grace in time of need</u>. First the president needs it, the secretary and the chairman of this convention and all the men who are at work to accomplish that for the good of our citizenship. We pray Thee that every one may have grace to the end, and may we remember Lord that the man who ruleth his own spirit is greater than the one who ruleth a city and therefore we can pray all together, the Lord's Prayer: "Our Father which art in heaven, hallowed be Thy name, Thy Kingdom come Thy will be done on earth as it is in heaven. Give us this day our daily bread and forgive our trespasses as we forgive those who trespass against us. Lead us not into temptation but deliver us from evil for Thine is the Kingdom and the Power and the Glory forever Amen.""

#12: *Pour Forth Thy Spirit upon Our Heads*

Tuesday morning, October 25, 1910 [p. 76, ***RACC***]:

"Gracious and All Wise Heavenly Father we thank Thee this morning for this beautiful day and for the health and the blessings that Thou hast pronounced upon us this day and that we have been permitted to walk again in the light of a new and beautiful day and to meet again for the duties of another session of the convention. We ask Thee to continue unto us all Thy mercies and blessings and take our hand in Thine for guidance and for safety in all the walks of life, and in all the acts of our lives. It has been said that in our getting, to get understanding and wisdom, [sic] <u>now Oh Lord it is our desire to get wisdom and to apply wisdom in all our acts but we need Thy Spirit to guide us and to assist us and we pray that Thou wilt pour forth Thy Spirit upon our heads and make us great and good people</u>, and when we have finished our world here on earth we would ask Thee to save us in Thy Kingdom above, is our wish and our supplication, in the name of Jesus Thine only Begotten Son, Amen."

#13: *Building the Foundations*

Wednesday morning, October 26, 1910 [p. 85, ***RACC***]:

"Oh Lord and Gracious Heavenly Father, we again thank Thee for our past blessings, of health, peace and happiness, and the privilege of meeting again in convention assembled, and we ask that Thou wouldst continue Thy mercies and blessings upon our heads through this day. Take us by the hand and lead us safely through the labors and tasks of another day, for we would not undertake this work without Thine aid and assistance. <u>In all the labors that are before us, we would that wisdom should be our guide and that our acts may be accounted unto us for good and for the good of this country and this great State which these men are now building the foundations. Lead us ever in the straight and narrow way and when we have finished our building and our work here on earth save us we pray Thee in Thy Kingdom above</u>, is our supplication in the Name of Thy Son Jesus Christ, our Savior, Amen."

#14: *Lead Us in the Straight and Narrow Pathways*

Thursday morning, October 27, 1910 [p. 92, ***RACC***]:

"Oh Lord our kind and gracious Heavenly Father, we thank Thee again this morning that we are alright, and that we are happy and that we have the privilege of meeting in another session of this Convention. Now Oh Father we desire that Thou wouldst bless the members of the Convention in their duties this day that whatever are the labors and duties of the day that they be given wisdom in the performance of those duties. <u>We need Thy blessings and Thy Guidance and we pray Thee Oh Lord to leave not alone, but lead us in the straight and narrow pathways in all our lives and keep and preserve us from danger, illness or sin</u>. We would thank Thee for the blessing of health and happiness, and the pursuit of pleasure and duties and that in our absence from our homes that our families are also granted that great blessing of health, so now Oh Lord we do commit ourselves and our lives into Thine Hand this day asking for Thy Holy Spirit to be with us always and to lead us in the narrow pathways of life to a home with Thee in Thy Kingdom above when we have finished our labors on earth. All these blessings we ask through the name of our Redeemer, Amen."

#15: *No Petty Petitions or Measures Incorporated*

Friday morning, October 28, 1910 [p. 98, ***RACC***]:

"Oh Lord, our God and Father of all, we have come together again in convention assembled and we desire to thank Thee for Thy mercies and Thy blessings, and to ask for Thy help and assistance in the labors of this day. In as much as these men are coming to the time when their work is very difficult and there are so many complications and measures that are perplexing to their minds and they desire wisdom in all their acts, therefore, we ask that they may have a rich blessing from Thine hand. Give unto them Thy Holy Spirit to guide the work of the convention and cause that not one of them will have any petty petitions or measures incorporated into the Constitution, but that each one may be disposed to act only for the very best good of the people and the State. <u>Oh Lord grant these men wisdom from above and grant that they may act with a purpose only to serve the people and the State and the great Nation</u>. These Blessings we would ask of Thee in the name of Thy Son Jesus, Amen."

#16: Bless These Men with Wisdom and Knowledge

Saturday morning, October 29, 1910 [p. 106, *RACC*]:

"Our Gracious Heavenly Father, and God of this great Universe, we thank Thee again this morning that we are alive and are again permitted to come to this place of business, without any illness or accidents having happened to any of these men. We thank Thee that Thou hast been so mindful of these men and the great labors they have to perform, that Thou hast blessed them with health and peace and a desire to faithfully perform the duties of the Convention, and now, <u>Oh Lord we would ask Thee to take them by the hand and lead them in the path of wisdom, and grant that they may serve Thee in serving the interests of Thy children. We would none of us attempt our duties in life without Thy help and Thine assistance and guidance in all our lives; therefore we pray Thee that Thou wouldst be ever mindful of us and lead us in the paths that Thou wouldst have us walk.</u> At the end of this third week of arduous labor and for the work that has been accomplished we thank Thee that all has been well with these men and now that the work is being brought to the committee of the whole for adoption in the Constitution, we ask that Thou wouldst specially bless these men with wisdom and knowledge in the great work that is before them to do. Lead us ever in the path of righteousness, and now Oh Lord after the manner of Thine only Begotten Son we would say, Our Father which are in heaven, hallowed be Thy name, Thy Kingdom come, Thy will be done on earth as it is in Heaven. Give us this day our daily bread, and forgive us our trespasses as we forgive those who trespass against us. Lead us not into temptation but deliver us from evil for Thine is the kingdom and the power and the glory forever, Amen."

#17: We Thank Thee that We are Still Alive

Monday morning, October 31, 1910 [p. 122, ***RACC***]:

"Almighty God, our Heavenly Father, <u>we thank Thee this morning that we are still alive, and that we are still probationers of hope on this side of the grave</u>, and we are still looking forward to the time when we shall be released. We thank Thee that there are no visible signs of Thy displeasure upon any of us. May God be upon us this day. This is about the period in the convention when reports will come in, and it may be that on some occasion we will be too hasty. <u>We pray Thee, therefore, that Thou wilt so rule in our hearts, as to overthrow those things which would be to our detriment, and bless the things which would be for our good</u>. May we not lose our temper in the heat of discussion and the interchange of thoughts. <u>Recognize the fact that we are all mortal beings; that we are frail, and do not understand things as the Divine Spirit, and do Thou therefore help us always[s] to have charity one toward another</u>. May our work be blessed. [All in unison] Our Father, who are in Heaven, hallowed be Thy name; Thy Kingdom come; Thy will be done on earth as it is in Heaven. Give us this day our daily bread, and forgive us our trespasses as we forgive those who trespass against us. Lead us not into temptation, but deliver us from evil. Amen."

#18: *We Acknowledge Thee as Our God and Leader*

Tuesday morning, November 1, 1910 [p. 136, ***RACC***]:

"Almighty Father, we bow our heads in Thy presence, this morning, and acknowledge Thee as our God and leader, and we would pray Thee to take hold of our hands and lead us this day. We might stumble and fall unless Thou walk by our side. See that we walk in the way Thou would have us go. May Thy blessing be upon us and our work. We may be criticized as to our labors and toil by men who do not understand, but we pray Thee, Lord, that the members of this convention may have nothing in this world in view but the good of Thy church and the good of the State in framing this constitution, so that when each one of them goes home, the people will say: "Well done, thou good and faithful servant." May the blessing of Heaven rest upon their families during their absence. And finally, when we are done with the toils, cares, and strife of this human life, lead us into the life eternal, and we will praise Thee forever and ever, Amen."

#19: *May There Be No Acrimony, Bickering or Strife*

Wednesday morning, November 2, 1910 [p. 153, ***RACC***]:

"Almighty God, our Heavenly Father, we thank Thee that our lives are preserved through the night, and that we are brought to see the light of this new day. That we are all gathered with the exception of two members, (fifty in number have answered their names.) Grant that everything we may and do may be said and done in furtherance of the great work in which we are engaged. We pray Thy blessing on the men who shall come to report today. May there be no acrimony, bickering or strife among us. We believe that most of these men here (nearly all in fact) are here for the good of their country at large, and <u>we pray Thee that the spirit of brotherly love may influence them for the good of this great state which we hope will be the brightest of the grant [sic, great] galaxy of states</u>. May Thy blessings rest upon them in the home and in their family relations, and in whatsoever pursuit they are following. Hear us in these our prayers this morning; forgive us our sins, for Christ's sake. Amen."

#20: *How Excellent is Thy Name in All the Earth*

Thursday morning, November 3, 1910 [p. 158, ***RACC***]:

"Oh Lord, our Lord, how excellent is Thy name in all the earth. Thou hast commanded men everywhere to pray, lifting up holy hands. We come before Thee with a keen sense of our unworthiness, and acknowledge Thee our God this morning, and pray for grace for the day. New responsibilities and new obligations are before us, and we know not what is this [sic, Thy] will concerning them, and we therefore pray that as we start forth on the labors and toils of the day we may have an opportunity to overthrow the obstacles. May the blessing of heaven come upon this body of men. May the blessings of our Heavenly Father richly be upon all appertaining [sic] to this constitutional convention. Forgive us our sins and guide us so that we attain Thy heavenly kingdom, and we will forevermore praise Thee. Amen."

#21: *May None Throw a Bomb in Our State*

Friday morning, November 4, 1910 [p. 174, ***RACC***]:

"Our gracious and heavenly Father, we thank Thee for the good rain which came last night to refresh the air, which is beneficial to both man and beast and all of the vegetable kingdom. We thank Thee that so many of us are alive. <u>We thank Thee that Thou hast not dealt with us according to our sins but according to the multitude of Thy mercy</u>. We thank Thee that we are still probationers of hope this side of the grave. Lord, we enter the duties of another day. It is suggested that we pray for one class of men. <u>We do not believe there is a single solitary man in this community who would turn so radical as to throw a bomb. We pray Thee therefore that there be no such thing in our State or in our capital or in this convention</u>. We do pray for the farmers here, that they have a good bank account; for the merchants, that they may have prosperity; for the mining man, that they may have a good lead; for the lawyers, that they may every one have a brief; for the physicians, that they may each have a patient; for the preachers, that they may have a pulpit. <u>Grant that in arranging and framing this constitution, it may meet the demands of all these classes of men, so that we may have a brotherhood in this proposed state</u>. We pray Thy blessing on our president, as he enters upon his duties, for during the hours of labor there may be some things come up in which he will need wisdom in all his rulings. Forgive us our sins, and at last in Heaven give us all a home, we ask in Jesus' name, Amen."

#22: *Surrounded By So Many Circumstances of Mercy*

Saturday morning, November 5, 1910 [p. 211, ***RACC***]:

"Oh Lord, our Heavenly Father, we thank Thee this morning that we are surrounded by so many circumstances of mercy, we thank Thee that Thou hast not dealt with us according to our sins, hast not rewarded us according to our iniquities, but that Thou hast spared our lives, and brought us here this morning under circumstances for which we thank Thee, and <u>we pray Thee that may not [sic] turn toward the right nor the left, but press toward the high calling</u>. Let Thy blessing come upon this body of men. All this we ask in the name of Him who taught us to pray and say: "Our Father who art in heaven, hallowed be Thy name; Thy kingdom come, Thy will be done on earth as it is in Heaven; Give us this day our daily bread and forgive us our sins as we forgive those who trespass against us. Lead us not into temptation but deliver us from evil, for Thine is the kingdom, the power, and the glory, for ever and ever. Amen.""

#23: All-Wise Heavenly Father

Monday morning, November 7, 1910 [p. 226, ***RACC***]:

"Our Gracious and All-Wise Heavenly Father, we feel to thank Thee again this morning for the light of a new day and the privilege of again meeting in Convention assembled. We thank Thee that we have been permitted to remain this side of the great Divide and that we have the blessing of health and happiness and for the hope we have of winning a crown when we have finished this probation below and have passed beyond the River. We would ask Thee Oh Lord that Thou wouldst give unto us Thy Holy Spirit this day for we would not begin the duties of another week without Thine assistance, and <u>therefore we place ourselves into Thy kind and protecting watch care knowing that Thou Art all merciful and Thou Art all Kind and Thy great love for Thy children here below will cause that great blessings will come to those who seek Thee asking such from Thee. We ask that these men may not [sic] do or say only that which would be for the great good of their State and their Country and that every act of this convention may be prompted by that love and the desire to serve their country and their constituents</u>. May they have nothing but the view of making a good and sound and a progressive constitution. Oh Lord may we all serve Thee faithfully to the end and when we have finished our work save us in Thy kingdom above, we ask Thee in the name of Thy Son our Redeemer, Amen."

#24: We Acknowledge Thy Divinity and Mightiness

Tuesday morning, November 8, 1910 [p. 238, *RACC*]:

"Once more we come before Thee Oh Lord our great and merciful heavenly Father and once more we ask of Thee for Thy mercies and Thy blessings and for guidance in this great work unto which we are called. Every one of these men from the members of the convention, the clerks and the pages need Thy help and Thy guidance in their labors that they have to perform and therefore we ask Thee Oh Lord to lead us, to take us by the hand for we indeed would place our hands in Thine and beseech Thee for all the blessings that Thou seest that we are in need of, for every task that we are to perform for Thy assistance we would ask. <u>We do acknowledge Thy divinity and Thy mightiness and we are grateful in our hearts for these blessings and with praise for Thy goodness and Thy kindness unto us we do ask that Thy Holy Spirit be with us to lead us aright that we may be ever found doing right and living the lives that Thou wouldst have Thy children live</u>. Grant that these men may write into this Constitution only that which will be for the best good of the people and that they may keep good their pledges unto the people. Now Oh Lord we do ask these blessings in the name of Thy Son, our only Redeemer. Amen."

#25: *May We Begin Right, Continue Right, and End Right*

Wednesday morning, November 9, 1910 [p. 247-248, *RACC*]:

"O Lord, our Heavenly Father, we thank Thee this morning that so many of us are alive and in health, and have been privileged to meet at this place where business is being transacted; and <u>we pray Thee, as we begin this day's work, every one of us, that we may begin right, and continue right, and end right, so that everything that is being done, and everything that shall be done, shall be done for the good of the greatest number of our fellow citizens</u>. O Lord, it has been whispered in our ears from two sources to pray for both the minority and the majority reports. <u>We have no concern in anything that is not for the glory of God and the good of the people to pray for; therefore, we pray that if the minority report be wrong, confound them, Lord, and make them so that they shall not pass. If the majority reports in anything be wrong, we pray Thee to confuse everything that will not be for the uplifting of the state of Arizona and for the good of the people that dwell therein. We pray Thee that these men may not have any selfish motives, or have anything in view of a personal interest. Help them, Lord, to have virtue enough to extend to the other party (the minority or the majority, as the case may be)—that they may have virtue enough to accord to them that which they claim for themselves. May they have nothing in view in this world but the good of the people of this great country, and may this country be a great country after they have framed a constitution.</u> And though the critics are suggesting what they ought to do, and what will become of the country if they do not do this, that, or the other thing. [sic] These critics would like very much to have the places of these men, but they could not fill them, Lord, if they had them. We pray Thee that these men may have faith and grace and courage enough to do the right thing, no difference what the critics may say. We pray Thy blessings upon these men today. They have hard work, both the President, and the Chairman of these committees, and those that have this conference in hand. Help them, Lord, to have clear vision and clear apprehension, and help us to pray, every one of us: Our Father, which art in Heaven, hallowed be Thy name; Thy Kingdom come, Thy will be done on earth as it is in Heaven. Give us our daily bread, and forgive us our trespasses as we forgive those that trespass against us; and lead us not into temptation, but deliver us from evil; for Thine is the kingdom, the power, and the glory, for ever and ever, Amen."

#26: *Stand on Record as Perpetuating Good Government*

Thursday morning, November 10, 1910 [p. 254-255, ***RACC***]:

"Our gracious Heavenly Father, we thank Thee that so many members of this convention are able to answer to the roll call this morning, and we have no news of any sorrow or misfortune of any of them or any of their loved ones, and we thank Thee that we are privileged to gather here for the business of this convention. We have come to the place where we are expecting something nice and good and crisp and short and pointed, in the way of a constitution. <u>We pray, Lord, that the people shall not be disappointed; that they may have a constitution that will be a credit—that will stand on record for ages to come as a constitution perpetuating good government for a good and useful territory or state</u>. We pray Thy blessing on every member of this constitutional convention. May Thy prosperity come upon all in their callings and professions, and may they be prosperous and happy and have a happy family. <u>We pray for the blessings of God on this Territory and on this incoming state. We pray that this may be one of the greatest and grandest states of the union, inasmuch as we have a good citizenship and a good set of men who are building up this country that it may be more and more inviting to the best class of emigration to come here</u>. We pray upon every man in his work today Thy blessings. There may be some difficulties and perplexities, and we pray they may have light to get through these dark places. We cannot expect perfection from imperfect beings, but we may have relative perfection, and we pray for it, and for the success of this convention until its close. Take hold of our hands and lead us. Hear us in these morning prayers, and forgive us our sins, and after this praise Thee for ever and ever. Amen."

James Crutchfield Leads the Lord's Prayer

Friday morning, November 11, 1910 [p. 270-271, ***RACC***]:

"Reverend (Seaborn) Crutchfield: Mr. President and gentlemen of the convention, allow me to substitute the younger Crutchfield for prayer this morning.

Reverend [James] Crutchfield: "Our Father who art in Heaven; hallowed be Thy name. Thy Kingdom come, Thy will be done on earth as it is in Heaven. Give us this day our daily bread, and forgive us our trespasses as we forgive those who trespass against us; and lead us not into temptation but deliver us from evil; for Thine is the kingdom, and the power, and the glory, forever and ever. Amen.""

#27: Oh Lord, Meet with Us Today

Saturday morning, November 12, 1910 [p. 288-289, ***RACC***]:

"Our gracious God and heavenly Father, we again approach Thee in the attitude of prayer and to thank Thee that Thou hast blessed us with wholesome minds and bodies and preserved us again to meet again for the duties of the convention. We are grateful to Thee for all Thy mercies and blessings and we would not attempt the labors of this day even the last day of the week without Thine assistance and Thy guidance; therefore we pray Thee <u>Oh Lord, that Thou wouldst meet with us today and abide with each and every member of the convention that they may be able to perform their labors with an eye single [sic] to the greatest good for the people of this State and for the common country. It matters not whether they be Democrat or Republican, Socialist or Populist they are here united for the same purpose and are desirous of doing good for the good of the State and the Nation and to represent their constituents in the great work of state building and would invoke Thine aid and assistance in all they may undertake, and as one in heart we would unite our voices in the Lord's Prayer</u>: Our Father who are in heaven, hallowed by Thy name; Thy kingdom come, Thy will be done on earth as it is in Heaven; give us this day our daily bread and forgive us our trespasses as we forgive those who trespass against us. Lead us not into temptation, but deliver us from evil for Thine is the kingdom and the power, and the glory forever, Amen."

#28: May Our Thoughts Be Acceptable in Thy Sight

Monday morning, November 14, 1910 [p. 308-309, ***RACC***]:

"Our gracious Lord, we thank Thee that we have had another Sunday of rest and refreshment and the privilege of going to the House of God to worship without distraction of mind, and that we are privileged this morning, so many of us to answer the roll call, even though it is on the second call. We thank God there are so many of us alive, and that no sorrowful news has reached our ears of any of our loved ones. Now a new week and a new day has dawned upon us, and we have new responsibilities and new obligations. We pray Thee Lord to lead us this day. We have come to the point in the convention now that work shall be dispatched rapidly, and we pray that the men may take the proper time, and that they may have studied so carefully, that they may have thoroughly digested all of the propositions that have come up, so <u>that they may send out a constitution to this State so that the people shall be satisfied and the world shall honor this convention because of the work they do</u>. We pray, therefore, this Monday morning that we may have the privilege of the presence and aid and assistance and comfort of God, so that we shall do the right thing and be restrained from doing the wrong. Let the blessing of God be upon these men and their families from whom they are separated. Let the good hand of God be upon the homes represented here this morning, and may each one be guided in the way of life everlasting. May the very thoughts of these men be acceptable in Thy sight, O Lord, our strength and our Redeemer. Help us to pray, one and all, from the last Page up to the President of this convention and say: Our Father, who art in Heaven; hallowed be Thy name. Thy kingdom come, Thy will be done on earth as it is in heaven. Give us this day our daily bread, and forgive us our trespasses as we forgive those who trespass against us, and lead us not into temptation but deliver us from evil; for Thine is the Kingdom, and the power and the glory, forever and ever. Amen."

#29: *Our Help Cometh from God*

Tuesday morning, November 15, 1910 [p. 342, ***RACC***]:

"Lord, Thou shalt hear our voices ascending high, to Thee we direct our prayers, to Thee lift up our eye[s]. <u>We lift up our eyes to Thy holy hill from whence cometh our help, for our help cometh from God</u>. All nature this morning rejoices, the trees, the singing birds and the lowing herds are all lifting their voices in praise to God this morning, and we ought, every one of us, to lift our voices in supplication to the God of our salvation this morning and return thanks for our preservation through the night and pray for a continuation of Thy mercies over us today. We want to have health and we have it and enjoy it this morning for which we thank God. We want these men to be strong in mind and body so that they shall be strong in all that they have to do and do the work gladly and cheerfully and willingly so that our fellow citizens may be blest by what they do, and so send a blessing upon every one of these men in their work. They have toils and cares that some of us do not understand. They need the spirit of God to lead them. <u>Oh Lord, forbid that any one man in this convention should take his cause out of Thy hands and undertake to run this business without the assistance of God</u>. Assist every man in his work so that he shall do it to the great good of our fellow citizens. This morning we all need Thy presence, we need all of us this morning to humbly bow our heads and pray: Our Father Who art in Heaven, hallowed be Thy name; Thy Kingdom come, Thy will be done on earth as it is in Heaven; Give us this day our daily bread and forgive us our trespasses as we forgive those who trespass against us; Lead us not into temptation, but deliver us from evil, for Thine is the kingdom, and the power and the glory forever. Amen."

#30: Showers from Heaven

Wednesday morning, November 16, 1910 [p. 391, ***RACC***]:

"We thank Thee our kind and gracious heavenly Father that we have been permitted to meet again this morning upon a new and beautiful day after the earth has been refreshed by the showers from heaven and for the good of this country.[sic] We thank Thee that Thou hast brought us forth this day in peace and happiness and in health to perform the duties and we ask that Thou wouldst guide the minds of these men to enact measures that will be only for the good of the State. Grant that they may have harmony and peace in their ranks and that they continue to make progress and that their labors may be finished within the time that they are so desirous of finishing them. <u>Cause that they may have the love of God and of men continually in their hearts and that they may not falter one inch</u>. Neither turn to the left or the right but continue in the straight and narrow way which leads all good men to the place of safety and brings them before their Maker. <u>Lead us Oh Lord in all the walks of life and leave us not alone for we are weak and erring but Thou alone art able and we place our hands in Thine for help and for guidance in every act of our lives</u> and we pray Thee Oh Lord to have mercy upon us and save us from evil and direct us to do good and save us in Thy kingdom above when we have finished our journey below, and all blessings we ask of Thee in the name of Thine only Begotten Son, our Redeemer, Amen."

#31: *The Rights of None Be Forgotten*

Thursday morning, November 17, 1910 [p. 410, ***RACC***]:

"Our gracious, heavenly Father we thank Thee for the rest of the past night and that we have been permitted to rise in health and strength for the labors of a new day. We thank Thee that none of these men are sick or in ill health and that they are present this morning to begin the labors of a new day. Now Oh Lord a new day is upon us and we would none of us undertake these duties until we have placed our hands in Thine and said, Oh Lord hold Thou our hands and lead us in the right path. Some men may have objections to some measures and things that are really for the best good of this work[;] now Oh Lord bless these men with wisdom and knowledge as to which course to pursue, for all the eyes of the people are looking this way. The people of this Territory, the people of the Nation, are looking this way. The politicians, the Democrats, the Republicans are looking this way. The Populists, and the Prohibitionists, and the suffragists are all looking this way, and the anti-Prohibitionists and the anti-suffragists are looking this way too. <u>Now Oh Lord grant that these men may no[t] commit any acts that they would be ashamed for these people whose eyes are turned this way to see and for the children and grandchildren of these men that they might not be ashamed to read the acts of their fathers in years to come. Cause that freedom of none shall be abridged nor the rights of none be forgotten, but that all people shall be given their freedoms and rights and that all acts done in this Convention shall be recorded for the good of this State and Nation</u> and now Oh Lord once again we ask Thee to take our hands this day and we in one harmonious voice do say: Our Father who art in Heaven, hallowed be Thy name. Thy kingdom come, Thy will be done on earth as it is in heaven. Give us this day our daily bread and forgive us our trespasses as we forgive those who trespass against us, and suffer us not to be led into temptation but deliver us from evil, for Thine is the Kingdom, and the power and the Glory, forever, Amen."

#32: O Lord, Give Audience Now as We Pray

Friday morning, November 18, 1910 [p. 431, ***RACC***]:

"O Lord, give audience now as we all pray: Our Father, who art in Heaven; hallowed be Thy name; Thy Kingdom come, Thy will be done on earth as it is in Heaven. Give us this day our daily bread, and forgive us our trespasses as we forgive those who trespass against us; and lead us not into temptation but deliver us from evil; for Thine is the kingdom, and the power, and the glory, forever and ever, Amen."

#33: *Great Cause of Liberty at Heart*

Saturday morning, November 19, 1910 [p. 460-461, ***RACC***]:

"<u>Our gracious heavenly Father we are commanded to always pray and to pray for all men everywhere, and this day we do lift up our voices in prayer for all men and for all people, but we especially pray for guidance this day among the men of this convention, those who have the making and arranging for a new state government, that they may have the great cause of liberty at heart and that they may be Godly men, men who love all mankind and will take no action save it be for the good of the people.</u> We pray that they may be men who will do something, men who have the interests of the state above all other interests and will seek only to adopt such measures as will be for the greatest amount of good for the people of the state. Oh Lord we have come to *the* place in this work where men are being tried and where they have many questions to decide and we pray Thee to give them wisdom and guidance in this work. <u>We have learned somewhere that when men do love their God and do call upon His name in Faith and with humble hearts, that they are lifted up to a higher and better life and now Oh Lord in this manner we do approach Thee and we do thank Thee for all Thy favors and blessings to us in the past and for the blessings of health and happiness.</u> We thank Thee that Thou hast spared the lives of these men and blessed them in their business affairs at home and in the health of their families, that no great sickness or sorrow has come to them, and we ask of Thee that Thy blessings shall so continue upon the men of this Convention, until their work is finished and throughout all the time and we ask these blessings all in the name of our Jesus, our Redeemer, Amen."

#34: *The Desert Shall Blossom as the Rose*

Monday morning, November 21, 1910 [p. 490-491, ***RACC***]:

"O Lord, our Heavenly Father, we thank Thee that on this bright Monday morning there are so many of us permitted to answer roll call as we enter upon the duties of another week and another day. We thank Thee for the spiritual strength that we got during the day yesterday for rest and refreshment for our souls to be refreshed and our minds to be relieved from the burden and tension and strain of business, and this morning we come into Thy presence in the beginning of the service and the session of the convention with clear minds and happy hearts and cheerful dispositions to do the work which is before us this day. Now Lord, we pray that these men who have failed to answer roll call this morning may not fail to be ready to answer roll call at the great time when all men shall be called upon to answer for their work done in this world. <u>We pray Thy blessings upon these men that they may have clear perceptions of duty and truth, and clear apprehension of that which they ought to do and may they do it with the hope that it shall be a great blessing to this country. We thank Thee for the hope that we have that some day this world will become like that which was prayed for and prophesied by a great prophet of old when the desert shall blossom as the rose. We pray that these men may have in their hearts and minds a disposition to bring about this great transformation, and to this end help them to formulate such laws as will be conducive to the extension of this very thing that was prayed for and hoped for. Let Thy blessing come upon us all.</u> We need each and every one of us this morning to pray the words Thou hast taught us to say: Our Father which are in Heaven, hallowed be Thy name, Thy Kingdom come, Thy will be done on earth as it is in Heaven. Give us this day our daily bread, and forgive us our trespasses as we forgive those who trespass against us, and lead us not into temptation but deliver us from evil; for Thine is the Power, and the Kingdom, and the Glory forever and ever. Amen."

#35: *Nothing but the Glory of God*

Tuesday morning, November 22, 1910 [p. 521, ***RACC***]:

"Oh, Lord, our Heavenly Father, we thank Thee when we see how unworthy we have been and how gracious Thou art to us; Thou has spared our lives and pardoned our mistakes. Thou hast dealt with us not according to our sins, but according to the multitude of Thy loving kindness, and this morning we feel like offering gratitude to Thee for His protecting guidance through the day. We would not undertake this day's work until we have put ourselves under the control of the Spirit. Control every expression of our lips, and every implementation of our minds. We pray Thee to give direction today to all that is said or done or thought by any of this constitutional convention membership so that they shall have the Spirit of Almighty God in the work they have in mind. <u>We pray they may have nothing but the glory of God and the love of their fellows in every pen that is driven, and every word spoken, and thought given or proposition offered so that they be under the control and guiding influence of Almighty God.</u> To pray Thy blessing on the men in the midst of this weekly work, and when we are all done with the turmoil of human life may we have a happy admittance to the Kingdom, we pray Thee in the Great Redeemer's name. Amen."

#36: *Very Keen Sense of Our Unworthiness*

Wednesday morning, November 23, 1910 [p. 571-572, ***RACC***]:

"O Lord, our Heavenly Father, we are brought under a sense of our dependence upon Thee this morning, and a very keen sense of our unworthiness, yet we know of no other source from which to derive strength only from Thee, and we come to Thee this morning and ask Thy guidance this day. May we be delivered from every evil thought and thing and expression this day. It is said "he that ruleth his own spirit is greater than he that taketh a city." We pray that every one of us may have rule over their spirits this day, so that we shall say nothing that would be contrary to Thy will and for our own good and the good of our fellow citizens. We pray Thy blessing upon this convention this morning. May every man be able to run the race with patience. Let Thy blessing come upon this whole convention and its work this day. We ask in our Great Redeemer's name. Amen."

#37: Thanksgiving Day

Thursday morning, November 24, 1910 [p. 619-620, ***RACC***]:

"Oh, Lord, our Heavenly Father, we thank Thee for the recurring of the annual day of Thanksgiving set apart by the great executive of our country and our state to give thanks to Almighty God for His providential care and His loving protection around and about us. We thank Thee, Lord, that we live in a Christian land where we can worship God under our own vines and fig trees, and that we can worship Thee without any restraint or inquisition. Thou hast taught us Thou art a powerful being and requirest worship from Thy people. We thank Thee that we are free from internal insurrection, free from war and pestilence. We thank Thee that we have sufficient food and raiment to provide for our bodily wants and for our soul. We thank Thee that Thy kind grace and providence has been along with us along from little boys through every danger, seen and unseen. May these men here today with one voice and one heart lift their voices to God with prayer and supplication, saying "Our Father, who art in Heaven, hallowed be Thy name. Give us this day our daily bread, and forgive us our trespasses as we forgive those who trespass against us. Lead us not into temptation, but deliver us from evil, for Thine is the kingdom, and the power, and the glory for ever and ever, Amen.""

#38: We Need Thee Every Hour

Friday morning, November 25, 1910 [p. 633-634, ***RACC***]:

"Oh Lord, our Heavenly Father, we come before Thee this bright new day to give to Thee our morning thanks and praise for the protection which has been ours through the night and brought us to the light of the new-born day.[sic] Now, Lord, we start out upon the duties and responsibilities and labors and toils of the day, and we would not dare to go in our own name and trusting in our own strength. We pray Thee, therefore, that we may have the guidance of the Spirit so that we may begin and continue in the way that will be good for us and for our people. We pray Thy blessing upon these men in the latter part of this convention; may they have acted and still act, in such a way that they shall have the approval of their conscience and the approval of the people who sent them to do this work. May they be able to go home and with confidence and trust look in the fact [sic, face] of their constituents and say, "We have done what you sent us to do. We are frail and make mistakes and do not do everything we should." Send Thy blessings on the men as they are gathered here. <u>We need Thee every hour, most gracious Lord, and while our faith looks up to Thee, Thou lamb of Calvary, we pray Thee that we may put our trust in Thee.</u> Send Thy blessing upon the homes of these men, their wives and children and their home interests. May the Good Father take care of them in their business. Guide us along life's perilous journey, and at the end lead us into Thy Kingdom. Amen."

#39: *Keep the Love of Freedom Ever Alive in Our Hearts*

Saturday morning, November 26, 1910 [p. 682, ***RACC***]:

"We that [sic, thank] Thee again this morning our heavenly Father that we are alive and that we have been permitted to meet again for the labors of the last day of the week. We thank Thee that Thou hast brought us together again in the flesh to meet face to face one with another and greet each other in love and peace, and we are glad that all is as favorable as it is. We ask Thee to be with us this day and grant a rich out-pouring of Thy Spirit upon these men that whatsoever they may do may be done righteously with the view of accomplishing good only. Bless them that the[y] may not be persuaded from doing right regardless of these men with measures and cause that their suggestions may not mean anything nor that they will be wielded for evil against the work of this convention. <u>Keep the love of liberty and freedom ever alive in our hearts and cause that nothing binding upon the just rights of men and institutions will ever be written into this constitution</u>. May we ever strive to live right so that when we are called by the Great Redeemer we may be prepared to meet the Judgments of a righteous God. Save us from sin, Oh Lord, and bring us back into Thy presence again, all of which we ask in the name of Jesus, Amen."

#40: *Public Sentiment Will Ultimately Be Adjusted*

Monday morning, November 28, 1910 [p. 714, ***RACC***]:

"Oh Lord we thank Thee this Monday morning that we are permitted to meet in this convention in health of body and mind. And now as we are in the last week of this convention in which many things will come up in review and as there might have been some things written in the constitution that ought not to have been written and some things left out that ought to have been put in. [sic] We pray that these men in their review of the past propositions may have sight on these subjects as to enable them to formulate a conservative constitution that our great country may look upon with approbation. <u>Oh Lord, we are not willing to believe President Taft will turn down our constitution on account of such a small matter as the Recall, Initiative and Referendum which is written in the constitution as the people of the great State of Arizona desire to be governed by</u>. Perhaps next week it will be on the headlines of all the newspapers in this territory and the country a [word unclear]… what the constitutional convention failed to do and what they ought to have done. But let none of us be alarmed; the question of women's suffrage is not dead, neither is the prohibition question dead, <u>but public sentiment will ultimately be adjusted in the course of time</u>. Now, Lord, give these men a measure of the Spirit to guide them on this work this week. And at last when we have all finished our work on earth, receive us all into heaven where we will praise Thee forever. Amen."

#41: *Thank You for the Privilege of Worshipping You*

Tuesday morning, November 29, 1910 [p. 751, ***RACC***]:

"O Lord our kind and merciful heavenly Father we thank Thee again for Thy blessing upon us this day and that we have been permitted to meet again in Convention assembled for the duties of another day. <u>We thank Thee for the blessings that surround us every day [,] for the privileges we have of worshiping Thee as the heart chooses</u> and we all in accord offer up this prayer: Our Father which art in heaven, hallowed be Thy name; Thy kingdom come, Thy will be done on earth as it is in heaven. Give us this day our daily bread and forgive us our trespasses as we forgive those who trespass against us, and lead us not into temptation, but deliver us from evil for Thine is the Kingdom and the Power and the Glory forever, Amen."

You May Write Your Own Prayer Here...

Wednesday morning, November 30, 1910 [p. 774, ***RACC***]:

[words not found]

Write your own prayer for good government for the leaders and state of Arizona here:

#42: *Wisdom Even to the End of This Great Labor*

Thursday morning, December 1, 1910 [p. 801-802, ***RACC***]:

"O Lord our heavenly Father we come before Thee this morning to make our wants known for we are told that if we do make our wants known they shall be granted if it be Thy will, for if we were left to ourselves for direction the doors of criticism are open for many men on the outside and perhaps some on the inside have said that we need not pray for our wants in this Convention. [sic] We are commanded *[to pray]* for what we need. Some papers have said that we need not pray for the men in business nor for food or raiment, but now O Lord we should pray for food and for raiment and offer thanks for them and we do this morning in this Convention pray for food and raiment whether Democrats or Republicans it make[s] no difference, for they are all deserving and they are all grateful for these blessings. If the soul is in close communication with the body, we should have our bodies comfortable so that the soul will be fed by a healthy body and mind, for the soul must have food, so therefore we ask for the comforts of life for all. <u>We pray for the merchants, the bankers, the doctors, the lawyers, and the cowmen, and for all classes of men, that they may be prepared to do their work and they might rely on Thee for help, but cause that they might not depend wholly on Thee, but that whatsoever they may have they may go to work and do it</u>. Now O Lord we are near the end of this Convention work and we would ask Thee to grant unto these men Thy Holy Spirit to guide them in all they may have to do to finish up this work, and that they may have wisdom even to the end of this great labor and that it may be acceptable to the people and to the parties who may have the approval of the Constitution for this State and as one in heart and mind and voice [we pray] the Prayer of Thy only Begotten Son: Our Father who art in Heaven, hallowed be Thy name, Thy kingdom come, Thy will be done on earth as it is in Heaven; give us this day our daily bread and forgive us our debts as we forgive those who trespass against us, and lead us not into temptation, but deliver us from evil for Thine is the Kingdom and the Power and the Glory forever, Amen."

#43: Forgive Us, O Lord, For Our Sins

Friday morning, December 2, 1910 [p. 829, ***RACC***]:

"O Lord our heavenly Father we thank Thee this morning that we are alive and that while we slumbered and slept that no harm came to us to mar our peace and our sweet slumbers, and that no sickness or death crept into our homes to take away our loved ones. We thank Thee that when we awoke this morning that we looked on the light of a new day and with thankful hearts we praise Thee for all Thy blessings and that when we arose from our slumbers that we are permitted to go forth in peace to our labors, while ma[n]y thousands have gone down to death. <u>Now, O Lord, we do thank Thee for all blessings for we know they all emanate from Thee and we ask that Thou wouldst guide us in all our walks of life and in every act of our lives. Keep us from doing wrong, and when any of us do commit those things which are wrong and are sorry and repentant, forgive us, O Lord, for our sins for we are weak and need Thee to lead us every day</u>. Inasmuch as we have once again met in this convention for the labors of finishing the framing of a constitution for a new State we would ask for Thy Holy Spirit to guide these men in all that they may do that they may adopt not one measure save it be for the good of the people and the state and the nations where in it might affect the Nation. [sic] We pray for the blessing of heaven to rest upon each and every member and let no one go astray. Now, O Lord, take us into Thy kind care and keeping [word unclear] save us from sin, forgive us when we do sin and when the end shall come save us all in Thy kingdom above. All blessings we ask in the name of Jesus. Amen."

#44: May Arizona Become One of the Fairest States

Saturday morning, December 3, 1910 [p. 847-848, ***RACC***]:

"Great God our heavenly Father we return unto Thee this morning our gratitude and thanks for the privilege we have of meeting once again in the convention to enter upon the duties and responsibilities that are ours to perform and we pray Thee that Thou wilt take charge of us this day and let Thy Spirit guide us in every act of the day. Take us by Thy hand and lead us in the straight and narrow way in all the walks of life. Now, O Lord, inasmuch as these men are about to complete the work of the framing of the constitution for the making of a great state we are willing that Thou should guide their minds to complete this work to the satisfaction of the members and without error, before they submit it to the people. If there is anything that they have omitted that should be included, inspire their minds to so place those things within that document, and if there are things written in the constitution that should not be there then give them such inspiration as to the amending it that it will be acceptable to the people and to the Congress of the United States. We pray Thee, O Lord, for all that is undone to have wisdom to do. <u>We pray Thee for the great State of Arizona that she may become one of the fairest states in the Union and for the great country in which we live do we pray and for all the people and nations grant that peace may ever abide with us.</u> We thank Thee that we are at peace with the world and that no wars or contentions are among our states or between us and other nations and we ask that these blessings continue upon us and that we shall lead lives of worthiness at all times in order that we may merit such blessings. Pardon us for all our sins and make us clean and holy before Thee, and all blessings we do ask of Thee in the name of Thy Son, our Redeemer. Amen."

#45: *We Dare Not Take One Step without Thy Aid*

Monday morning, December 5, 1910 [p. 877, ***RACC***]:

"O Lord, our Heavenly Father, we thank Thee that Thou hast preserved us through another Sabbath day and through another night, and that we are brought together this morning under circumstances of so much mercy. And now, Lord, as we enter upon the labors and duties of the last week, perhaps, of this constitutional convention, we should not undertake the work of this week until we have put ourselves under Thy controlling influence, and we pray Thee to guide us this day for Thy Name's sake. We pray Thee, O Lord, if we have done anything wrong up to this day of the convention, we are heartily sorry for it. If it is possible, if we have done anything wrong, for us to right it, help us to right up everything wrong we may have done. If we have neglected to do some things we ought to have done, help us to try to do the right thing the balance of this week, so that these men shall send out this constitution to the people for endorsement or rejection, and, <u>O Lord, we pray that they may have such a constitution as the people will endorse, and they will feel that the confidence they have put in these men in sending them here to frame this constitution has not been betrayed, and may it be such a constitution that we may all be proud of it</u>. This morning, Lord, we need Thee. We dare not take one step without Thy aid. Hold Thou our hands, Lord, so when each of us reaches the margin of that dark river Thou didst cross for us we may find the crossing bright, and when we have wrought Thy will and each one of us has accomplished that whereunto Thou hast sent us into the world, save us in Thy kingdom above, and we will praise Thee forever and ever. Amen."

#46: *Now Help Us to Pray*

Tuesday morning, December 6, 1910 [p. 904-905, ***RACC***]:

"We thank Thee, our gracious Heavenly Father, for the health we enjoy this morning, and for this new day, and for the blessings that surround us this morning. We come to Thee this morning to ask Thee for the things which we so much need. May we have Thy help to aid us in all that we undertake to do. And now help us to pray: Our Father, who art in heaven, hallowed be Thy name. Thy kingdom come, Thy will be done on earth as it is in Heaven. Give us this day our daily bread and forgive us our trespasses [as] we forgive those who trespass against us. And lead us not into temptation, but deliver us from evil, for Thine is the kingdom, and the power and the glory for ever and ever. Amen."

#47: *Take All Our Sins Away*

Wednesday morning, December 7, 1910 [p. 924, ***RACC***]:

"We thank Thee this morning our Heavenly Father, that we are alive and that we have health of body and health of mind, and have a disposition of heart to call upon our Lord. And now Lord we call upon Thee this morning. <u>Hear us as we pray, and take all our sins away, and from this day may we be wholly Thine</u>. Send upon us Thy grace for the day's duties and responsibilities and labors. We would not undertake anything until we have first invoked the Divine Presence to guide us in all our ways and in all our thoughts and in all our fellow men. Send a blessing to these men in these closing hours of the convention. May they have a conscious void of offense toward Thee and toward their fellow men, and when they have done their work may they have the assurance that they have done that which they have been sent here to do. Hear us; take away our sins; and when the fitful scenes of life are over, save us all in Heaven. We ask all in the Great Redeemer's name. Amen."

#48: That We Shall Have a Clean and Good Constitution

Thursday morning, December 8, 1910 [p. 959-960, ***RACC***]:

"O Lord, our Heavenly Father, we thank Thee that we have come to this hour. For these sixty days these men have been gathering here day after day in this work, and we are permitted to gather here at the last day allotted to them in which to do the work which they have come here to do. We thank Thee, Lord, that none of these men have been caused to die; no sorrow nor sadness has come to any of their homes that is giving them great distress. We thank Thee for the merciful circumstances by which they are surrounded today, and we thank Thee, Lord, that we have the disposition of heart to call upon God, and we pray Thee, Lord, to be with every one of these men this day. We thank Thee, Lord, that there is enough patriotism in these men, though they may not get pay for the labors they have to do in the future to write up this constitution, that they have patriotism to come here a day and work gratuitous, and <u>we pray Thee that they may have courage to do manfully what ought to be done before they adjourn, so that they shall have a clean and a good constitution written</u>. Lord, we thank Thee for our association with these men for these sixty days. We thank Thee for the absence of [word unclear] we have heard—but little—and for the cleanness of these members' conversation and in life. We thank Thee that as representatives of the people they express a high type of Christian civilization and [words unclear] gentility and manliness. We pray Thee that it may characterize them through their lives, and their families and friends with whom they are associated and over whom they have an influence, that they may be influenced to the right that they shall be honorable citizens and fellow citizens of this great country. Hear us, Lord, in these our morning prayers. Forgive us our sins. Lead us along the way of life gently, smoothly and sweetly, and in Heaven give us a home. We ask in the Great Redeemer's name. Amen."

#49: All Sing "America", Approval of God and Men

Friday morning, December 9, 1910 [p. 1001, ***RACC***]:

"Mr. President and gentlemen of the convention, let us sing a verse of our national hymn. (Convention sings "America".)

O Lord, our God, we thank Thee this morning for the patriotic feeling that is in our hearts this morning as we enter upon this new day, and we pray Thee, Lord, to guide us in all we do and say this day, for Thy Name's sake. Bless these men as they are closing up the work of this convention. May they, as they start to their homes, may they find no sorrow in their homes. <u>May they find everything conducive to their happiness in this life, preparatory for their happiness in the life which is to come</u>. And, O Lord, we pray that they may be as patriotic in trying to bring about the adoption of this constitution as they have been in framing it, as careful, as honest, as earnest, as solicitous as they have been for these sixty-one days. And, O Lord, our God, may it be in the hearts of the people to adopt this constitution. While there are some who think there are some things that ought not to have been put in it, and others think there are too many things in it, but we pray Thee, Lord, as according to our different views and interests in this territory these men have come to the conclusion that they have made a conservative constitution, that the people may adopt it. Give these men favor in the sight of the people. Give them favor in the sight of their constituents, and <u>give us all favor with Thee, so that we shall have the approval of God and of men</u>. Our Father, who art in Heaven; hallowed be Thy name; Thy kingdom come, Thy will be done, on earth as it is in Heaven; give us this day our daily bread and forgive us our trespasses as we forgive those who trespass against us; Lead us not into temptation, but deliver us from evil, for Thine is the kingdom and the power and the glory, forever. Amen."

#50: *Dismiss Us, Lord, With Thy Blessing*

Friday afternoon, December 9, 1910 [p. 1011, ***RACC***]:

"Mr. Morgan: Mr. President, I move we extend a vote of thanks to our excellent chaplain, Mr. Crutchfield.
(applause)
Mr. President: Gentlemen of the convention, the gentleman from Mohave, Mr. Morgan, has moved a vote of thanks to our excellent chaplain; the Reverend Crutchfield. Those in favor of that motion will answer "aye;" those opposed will answer "no."
The "ayes" have it.
[Signing of Constitution with list of signers]
"attested by A. W. Cole, Secretary Constitutional Convention; signed and sealed by Geo. U. Young, Secretary and Acting Governor of the Territory of Arizona."
Mr. President: Gentlemen of the convention, the document has been signed. As we opened the exercises of the day with the singing of the national anthem, I think it would be only fitting that we close the exercises by singing a verse of "America," and then the chaplain will invoke the benediction.
Members sing "America."

Reverend Crutchfield: "Our Father, we are about to disband, separate, part, go to our different homes. O Lord, go with every one of these men and all these attaches and these little boys and girls. Do Thou accompany them to their homes. And these men who will have this labor on their hands for these weeks and months, bless them in all their proceedings in life. Dismiss us, Lord, with Thy blessing. Help us to say: Our Father who art in Heaven, hallowed by Thy name. Thy kingdom come, Thy will be done on earth as it is in Heaven. Give us this day our daily bread, and forgive us our trespasses as we forgive those that trespass against us. And lead us not into temptation, but deliver us from evil, for Thine is the Kingdom, and the Power, and the Glory, for ever and ever. Amen."

Constitutional Convention adjourned sine die.

IX. Preamble to the Constitution

"We, the people of the state of Arizona, grateful to Almighty God for our liberties, do ordain this constitution."

The preamble is defined as the opening statement of the primary legal document of a government entity. Thus, it carries particular weight in its declaration. The above Preamble to the Arizona Constitution was adopted unanimously by a vote of 46-0 on December 6, 1910 of the *Constitutional Convention for the statehood of Arizona* [p. 905 **RACC**]. During the course of the Constitutional Convention the Preamble underwent several revisions. James Crutchfield, the son of Chaplain Seaborn Crutchfield, served as the Preamble Committee Chairman.

James Crutchfield was a graduate of Vanderbilt and himself a Methodist minister, a Democrat delegate from Maricopa County, and he would later serve 20 years as chaplain for the state House of Representatives. He died in 1957 at the age of 86 [p. 1389 **RACC**].

The first draft (Proposition No. 1 of the Constitutional Convention) of the Preamble proposed on the 6th day of the Convention by the Committee of the Preamble, presented by Committee Chairman James Crutchfield, was as follows:

> *"We, the People of Arizona, invoking the guidance of the Supreme Being, do ordain and establish this Constitution in order to perpetuate liberty and justice in our state, and provide for the peace and welfare of posterity."* [p. 41, **RACC**]

From this draft the Committee of the Preamble made revisions until arriving at the final version adopted unanimously. The approved Preamble (Proposition No. 5 of the Constitutional Convention) was formally introduced by Mr. Albert C. Baker, of Maricopa County.

Briefly, Albert Cornelius Baker (1845-1921) was born in Alabama, served in the Confederate Army, became a lawyer, and practiced law in three California cities before moving to Arizona in 1879 for the rest of his life. He went on to serve as Maricopa County attorney, Phoenix city attorney, Chief Justice of Arizona Territory (1893-1897), and Justice of the Arizona Supreme Court 1919-1921 [p. 1387, *RACC*].

Interestingly, the Arizona Territorial legislature of 1891 also went through the arduous process of completing a constitutional convention and producing a constitution for statehood (which was obviously not ratified by the federal government at the time). However, there is little doubt that the effort in 1891 did make contributions to the convention of 1910, both in language and in practice.

Here is the Preamble of the *Arizona Constitutional Convention of 1891* (signed October 2, 1891):

"We, the people of Arizona, grateful to the Supreme Being for our liberties, in order to form a more independent and perfect government, establish justice, insure domestic tranquility, provide for the common defense, promote the general welfare, and secure the blessings of liberty to ourselves and our posterity, do ordain and establish this Constitution for the State of Arizona."

As with each effort by Arizona's founders, the Preamble of every state of the Union also directly acknowledges God. Again, we see that we live in a nation who prominently, even as a first order of business, recognizes Almighty God in our foundational documents of government.

Here is a listing of the constitutional acknowledgments of God in the Preambles of all fifty United States of America along with the year they were approved:

Alabama 1901, Preamble: We, the people of the State of Alabama, invoking the favor and guidance of Almighty God, do ordain and establish the following Constitution…

Alaska 1956, Preamble: We, the people of Alaska, grateful to God and to those who founded our nation and pioneered this great land…

Arizona 1911, Preamble: We, the people of the State of Arizona, grateful to Almighty God for our liberties, do ordain this Constitution...

Arkansas 1874, Preamble: We, the people of the State of Arkansas, grateful to Almighty God for the privilege of choosing our own form of government...

California 1879, Preamble: We, the People of the State of California, grateful to Almighty God for our freedom…

Colorado 1876, Preamble: We, the people of Colorado, with profound reverence for the Supreme Ruler of Universe...

Connecticut 1818, Preamble: The People of Connecticut, acknowledging with gratitude the good Providence of God in permitting them to enjoy…

Delaware 1897, Preamble: Through Divine Goodness all men have, by nature, the rights of worshipping and serving their Creator according to the dictates of their consciences…

Florida 1885, Preamble: We, the people of the State of Florida, grateful to Almighty God for our constitutional liberty, establish this Constitution...

Georgia 1777, Preamble: We, the people of Georgia, relying upon protection and guidance of Almighty God, do ordain and establish this Constitution...

Hawaii 1959, Preamble: We, the people of Hawaii, Grateful for Divine Guidance... establish this Constitution…

Idaho 1889, Preamble: We, the people of the State of Idaho, grateful to Almighty God for our freedom, to secure its blessings…

Illinois 1870, Preamble: We, the people of the State of Illinois, grateful to Almighty God for the civil, political and religious liberty which He hath so long permitted us to enjoy and looking to Him for a blessing on our endeavors…

Indiana 1851, Preamble: We, the People of the State of Indiana, grateful to Almighty God for the free exercise of the right to choose our form of government…

Iowa 1857, Preamble: We, the People of the State of Iowa, grateful to the Supreme Being for the blessings hitherto enjoyed, and feeling our dependence on Him for a continuation of these blessings establish this Constitution...

Kansas 1859, Preamble: We, the people of Kansas, grateful to Almighty God for our civil and religious privileges establish this Constitution...

Kentucky 1891, Preamble: We, the people of the Commonwealth, are grateful to Almighty God for the civil, political and religious liberties…

Louisiana 1921, Preamble: We, the people of the State of Louisiana, grateful to Almighty God for the civil, political and religious liberties we enjoy...

Maine 1820, Preamble: We, the People of Maine, acknowledging with grateful hearts the goodness of the Sovereign Ruler of the Universe in affording us an opportunity ... And imploring His aid and direction...

Maryland 1776, Preamble: We, the people of the state of Maryland, grateful to Almighty God for our civil and religious liberty...

Massachusetts 1780, Preamble: We...the people of Massachusetts, acknowledging with grateful hearts, the goodness of the Great Legislator of the Universe... in the course of His Providence, an opportunity and devoutly imploring His direction...

Michigan 1908, Preamble: We, the people of the State of Michigan, grateful to Almighty God for the blessings of freedom establish this Constitution...

Minnesota, 1857, Preamble: We, the people of the State of Minnesota, grateful to God for our civil and religious liberty, and desiring to perpetuate its blessings...

Mississippi 1890, Preamble: We, the people of Mississippi in convention assembled, grateful to Almighty God, and invoking His blessing on our work...

Missouri 1845, Preamble: We, the people of Missouri, with profound reverence for the Supreme Ruler of the Universe, and grateful for His goodness...

Montana 1889, Preamble: We, the people of Montana, grateful to Almighty God for the blessings of liberty establish this Constitution...

Nebraska 1875, Preamble: We, the people, grateful to Almighty God for our freedom...

Nevada 1864, Preamble: We, the people of the State of Nevada, grateful to Almighty God for our freedom establish this Constitution...

New Hampshire 1792, Part I. Art. I. Sec. V: Every individual has a natural and unalienable right to worship God according to the dictates of his own conscience...

New Jersey 1844, Preamble: We, the people of the State of New Jersey, grateful to Almighty God for civil and religious liberty which He hath so long permitted us to enjoy, and looking to Him for a blessing on our endeavors...

New Mexico 1911, Preamble: We, the People of New Mexico, grateful to Almighty God for the blessings of liberty...

New York 1846, Preamble: We, the people of the State of New York, grateful to Almighty God for our freedom, in order to secure its blessings...

North Carolina 1868, Preamble: We, the people of the State of North Carolina, grateful to Almighty God, the Sovereign Ruler of Nations, for our civil, political, and religious liberties, and acknowledging our dependence upon Him for the continuance of those...

North Dakota 1889, Preamble: We, the people of North Dakota, grateful to Almighty God for the blessings of civil and religious liberty, do ordain...

Ohio 1852, Preamble: We, the people of the state of Ohio, grateful to Almighty God for our freedom, to secure its blessings and to promote our common...

Oklahoma 1907, Preamble: Invoking the guidance of Almighty God, in order to secure and perpetuate the blessings of liberty...

Oregon 1857, Bill of Rights, Article I. Section 2: All men shall be secure in the Natural right, to worship Almighty God according to the dictates of their consciences...

Pennsylvania 1776, Preamble: We, the people of Pennsylvania, grateful to Almighty God for the blessings of civil and religious liberty, and humbly invoking His guidance...

Rhode Island 1842, Preamble: We, the People of the State of Rhode Island, grateful to Almighty God for the civil and religious liberty which He hath so long permitted us to enjoy, and looking to Him for a blessing...

South Carolina, 1778, Preamble: We, the people of he State of South Carolina, grateful to God for our liberties, do ordain and establish this Constitution...

South Dakota 1889, Preamble: We, the people of South Dakota, grateful to Almighty God for our civil and religious liberties...

Tennessee 1796, Art. XI.III: That all men have a natural and indefeasible right to worship Almighty God according to the dictates of their conscience...

Texas 1845, Preamble: We, the People of the Republic of Texas, acknowledging, with gratitude, the grace and beneficence of God...

Utah 1896, Preamble: Grateful to Almighty God for life and liberty, we establish this Constitution...

Vermont 1777, Preamble: Whereas all government ought to enable the individuals who compose it to enjoy their natural rights, and other blessings which the Author of Existence has bestowed on man...

Virginia 1776, Bill of Rights, XVI: Religion, or the Duty which we owe our Creator can be directed only by Reason and that it is the mutual duty of all to practice Christian Forbearance, Love and Charity towards each other...

Washington 1889, Preamble: We, the People of the State of Washington, grateful to the Supreme Ruler of the Universe for our liberties, do ordain this Constitution...

West Virginia 1872, Preamble: Since through Divine Providence we enjoy the blessings of civil, political and religious liberty, we, the people of West Virginia reaffirm our faith in and constant reliance upon God...

Wisconsin 1848, Preamble: We, the people of Wisconsin, grateful to Almighty God for our freedom, domestic tranquility...

Wyoming 1890, Preamble: We, the people of the State of Wyoming, grateful to God for our civil, political, and religious liberties... establish this Constitution...

An interesting anomaly provides for the following trivia question:

"Which is the only constitutional preamble in the United States that does not directly acknowledge God?"

ANSWER: The Preamble (or opening statement) of the *U.S. Constitution* of 1787!

The *U.S. Constitution* followed the *Declaration of Independence* and at least seven state constitutional preambles, and many other earlier documents of the colonies, all of which reference God. *So why would God not be mentioned in the Preamble of the U.S. Constitution?* It may be that at least part of the answer lies in the singular focus of the writers to declare unequivocally that the United States of America would be a government of the people, by the people, and for the people, and not a kingship or similar form of government.

"We the People of the United States, in Order to form a more perfect Union, establish Justice, insure domestic Tranquility, provide for the common defense, promote the general Welfare, and secure the Blessings of Liberty to ourselves and our Posterity, do ordain and establish this Constitution for the United States of America."
– Preamble, U.S. Constitution

X. Arizona State Seal and Motto

"Ditat Deus: God Enriches"

While the Preambles of all states unanimously honor God, Arizona joins only eight other states that directly or indirectly name God in their state motto.

Florida shares our national motto, *"In God we trust"*, Ohio: *"With God all things are possible"*, Colorado: the Latin expression for *"Nothing without Providence"* (or *"Nothing without the Diety"*), Connecticut: *"He who transplanted still sustains"*, Maine: *"I direct"*, South Dakota: *"Under God the people rule"*, and Kentucky recently added a new Latin motto in 2002 meaning, *"Let us give thanks to God"* to go with their original English motto of *"United we stand, divided we fall."*

The Arizona motto is the Latin *"Ditat Deus"* which is generally translated *"God Enriches."* This motto has been ours since the beginning of our territorial government and by all accounts accredited to Arizona's first territorial secretary, Richard C. McCormick.

I have found no record of why Secretary McCormick may have chosen this Latin expression as part of the State Seal, other than it appears he came prepared with a territorial seal design, which included the motto, before or during his travels with the governmental party to Arizona in late 1863. He knew that he would need a seal as part of his duties to provide official authorization of territorial government documents.

Prior to his appointment by President Lincoln as the territorial secretary, McCormick edited the *Young Men's Magazine* in 1858-1859, the publication for the *YMCA—Young Men's Christian Association*, which would seem to be indicative of his faith, particularly in that era.

Richard Cunningham McCormick (1832-1901)
First Secretary of the Arizona Territory and Second Governor
Portrait c.1864, public domain

Along with the territorial seal and motto, McCormick also brought the first printing press to Arizona and started the first newspapers of the territory, the *Arizona Miner* in Prescott in 1864, and the *Arizona Citizen* in Tucson in 1870. After Governor John Goodwin was elected territorial delegate of Arizona, McCormick was appointed as the second governor of the Arizona Territory by President Andrew Johnson in 1866. Sadly, in 1867 Richard McCormick lost his wife Margaret after she delivered a stillborn child, just a year and a half after they were married. She was the first "First Lady" who lived in Arizona.

On the afternoon of November 25, 1910 during the Constitutional Convention for the statehood of Arizona, there was floor discussion about the state Seal and Motto that reflects back upon its history:

"Mr. Cuniff: ...I want to put before the convention a suggestion for a seal, which has been suggested by Mr. E.E. Motter of Phoenix... On this matter it may be of interest if I read some data which has been furnished by the Arizona historian, Miss [Sharlot] Hall:

"The first legislature of Arizona, in session at Prescott from the 26th of September to the 10th of November [1864] passed the following act creating an official seal: 'An Act creating a seal for the Territory of Arizona. Be it enacted by the Legislative Assembly of the Territory of Arizona: Section 1. The seal of this Territory shall be of the size of two and one quarter inches in diameter and of the following design: A view of the San Francisco Mountains in the distance, with a deer, pine trees, and a columnar cactus in the foreground; the motto to be 'Ditat Deus'. The date of the said seal to be 1863, the year of the organization of the Territory... Approved November 9, 1864.'

Among pioneers and by some writers of the early seventies [1870s] this seal was called the 'Baking Powder Seal' from the fact that the design was almost an exact duplicate of the picture seen upon the Pioneer Baking Powder and Spices then very generally used in the country and prepared and packed by Folger of San Francisco..."

[Mr. Cuniff continues...] *"The following extract from "Adventures in Apache Country, a Tour Through Arizona and Sonora," by J. Ross Browne, published by Harper and Brothers in 1869 will also be of interest: (page 27) "Let us take a look at the official seal of the Territory designed by Mr. Secretary McCormick: An honest miner stands with his left hand in his pocket feeling for the profits of his day's labor. The expression of his countenance is indicative of a serious frame of mind; he gazes into the future, and sees gold and silver a long way off. His spade stands ready to dig it and his wheelbarrow to wheel it. In the background you see the two prominent peaks of Bill Williams' mountain, where he contemplates prospecting next year; or possibly these may be dirt piles which he has already thrown up, and not yet washed for lack of water. The appropriate motto is 'Ditat Deus."*

[Mr. Cuniff continues...] In reference to this seal there is a pun "'God reigns' in Arizona—even in dry weather." Now it has been taken for granted that this motto means "God reigns," but I have looked up the meaning of this verb and find the meaning is "enriches." [pp. 650-651, The Records of the Arizona Constitutional Convention of 1910, edited by John S. Goff]

Whether Arizona's Latin motto of *Ditat Deus* was originally adopted by Arizona's Territorial government in 1864 with the idea that it meant *"God reigns"* is certainly interesting to consider due to this direct recognition of God's authority in government, but we may not definitively know. Regardless, either intended translation honors God.

In fact, the translation *"God enriches"* also makes sense considering the primary industry of mining during that era and in the context of the Territorial Seal design that McCormick brought with him to Arizona.

A few historical reviews suggest that Genesis 14:23 may be the inspiration for the motto, which does incorporate the correct "enriches" translation of *Ditat*. You may wish to read Genesis, chapter 14 to get the context. In this passage, the Old Testament patriarch Abraham (actually Abram before he was named Abraham by God) makes the following statement when he turns down the offer of a reward for rescuing a king and his people out of the hands of their enemies:

"But Abram said to the king of Sodom, "I have raised my hand to the Lord, God Most High, the Possessor of heaven and earth, that I will take nothing, from a thread to a sandal strap, and that I will not take anything that is yours, lest you should say, 'I have made Abram rich.'""
– Genesis 14:22-23

Abram is declaring that he would not take the reward offered, which under the protocol of that time would have been considered appropriate, but he wanted only to be known as being enriched by God. That is a powerful statement of acknowledgment and dependence on God, and for me, provides an additional basis for a most noble State Motto.

I find it very interesting that this passage also includes Abram swearing an oath before God (v. 22) just as we would see a government official being sworn into office today (see p. 60-63). The literal Hebrew rendering for this verse is *"I have raised my hand and sworn an oath to the Lord God Most High..."* Thus, Abram is affirming and adhering to the oath perhaps only he and God knew he had made prior to his victory.

The Latin word used for "enriches" in Genesis 14:23 is actually *ditavi* in the Latin Vulgate Bible (Jerome, 405AD). Though it is a derivative of the same root word as *ditat*, the Latin *ditat* itself is only found in one verse—in 1 Samuel 2:7.

> *"The Lord makes poor and makes rich [ditat]; He brings low and lifts up." – 1 Samuel 2:7*

The original Hebrew word which is translated *ditat* in the Latin Vulgate is *'ashar*. There are a few other verses in addition to Genesis 14:23 and 1 Samuel 2:7 in which the Hebrew word *'ashar* also appear that further develop the theme of 'God enriches':

> *"You visit the earth and water it; You greatly enrich ['ashar] it; the river of God is full of water; You provide their grain, for so You have prepared it." – Psalm 65:9*

> *"The blessing of the Lord makes one rich ['ashar], and He adds no sorrow with it." – Proverbs 10:22*

In Psalm 65, particularly verses 9-13, it is uncanny how it describes much of the background of the current Arizona State Seal, with *"God enriches"* written in it! I provide the Psalm 65 passage and the legal description below, so that you can easily compare them:

> *"You visit the earth and water it, You greatly enrich it; the river of God is full of water [a storage reservoir?]; You provide their grain, for so You have prepared it. You water its ridges abundantly [irrigated fields], You settle its furrows; You make it soft with showers, You bless its growth. You crown the year with Your goodness, and Your paths drip with abundance. They drop on the pastures of the wilderness, and the little hills rejoice on every side. The pastures are clothed with flocks [cattle grazing]; the valleys also are covered with grain; they shout for joy, they also sing."*

Here is the current full language for the Arizona Seal and Motto in the *Constitution of the State of Arizona*:

> ARTICLE XXII—*Schedule and Miscellaneous*
> Section 20: *The seal of the State shall be of the following design: In the background shall be a range of mountains, with the sun rising behind the peaks thereof, and at the right side of the range of mountains there shall be a storage reservoir and a dam, below which in the middle distance are irrigated fields and orchards reaching into the foreground, at the right of which are cattle grazing. To the left in the middle distance on a mountain side is a quartz mill in front of which and in the foreground is a miner standing with pick and shovel. Above this device shall be the motto: "Ditat Deus." In a circular band surrounding the whole device shall be inscribed: "Great Seal of The State of Arizona", with the year of admission of the State into the Union.*

There was more than a little discussion about the description of the State Seal during the Constitutional Convention of 1910. On one hand, some argued to keep the territorial seal unchanged—'It was good enough then, so it is good enough now.' Others adamantly wanted to make changes indicative of a new image for the state. After the dust cleared, the vote was for a new seal. However, I have found no discussions about changing the motto of Arizona. *Ditat Deus* seems to have had a fixed place in Arizona history since its inception in 1863.

The actual artwork of the Seal has changed many times over the years. Some of these renderings have accurately followed the written legal description, while some designs strayed by leaving out or changing some design components. Through every change, the Arizona motto *Ditat Deus* has always been included.

Following is the first Arizona Territorial Seal provided by Richard McCormick and then the current Arizona State Seal. See the website of the Arizona Secretary of State Jan Brewer for more information: www.azsos.gov/Info/state_seal/history.

Original territorial seal of 1863
Courtesy of the Arizona Secretary of State website:
www.azsos.gov/Info/state_seal/history

Current Arizona State Seal
Courtesy of the Arizona Secretary of State website:
www.azsos.gov/Info/state_seal/history

XI. Arizona Statehood – 1912

"A frequent recurrence to fundamental principles is essential to the security of individual rights and the perpetuity of free government."
—Article II, Section 1, Arizona Constitution

After 50 years of territorial status with direct oversight and control by the federal government (including the power to appoint the governor), at last, on Valentine's Day, February 14, 1912, at 10:00am in Washington, D.C., President William Howard Taft signed the proclamation for Arizona statehood. The news was immediately telegrammed to Phoenix. Later that day, with his hand on a Bible, George W. P. Hunt was sworn in as the first governor of the state of Arizona.

Immediately after the oath of office was administered, Chaplain Seaborn Crutchfield gave the invocation. In the excitement of the celebration of this ceremony, this inaugural prayer does not appear to have been recorded.

Statehood itself meant the immediate adoption of the *Constitution of the State of Arizona*. Following the Preamble and Article I concerning "State Boundaries" is the "Declaration of Rights" outlined in Article II. Below are the first four of 34 sections of Article II:

> *Section 1. A frequent recurrence to fundamental principles is essential to the security of individual rights and the perpetuity of free government.*
>
> *Section 2. All political power is inherent in the people, and governments derive their just powers from the consent of the governed, and are established to protect and maintain individual rights.*
>
> *Section 3. The Constitution of the United States is the supreme law of the land.*

Section 4. No person shall be deprived of life, liberty, or property without due process of law.

The *Article II, Section 1* paragraph resonates with the very purpose of this book. It *is* good to refer back to our fundamental principles—even essential. Most fundamental of all is our frequent acknowledgement of our dependence and thanksgiving to God.

These first four sections display the language of the foundations of good government being carried forward through our national heritage.

Statehood brings "equal footing" with all states. It links each state under the *Constitution of the United States*, with all the rights, restrictions, and privileges that infers. The form and principles of our *Arizona State Constitution* clearly demonstrate its place in the stream of American governmental history infused with the mark of God.

The document itself is not fancy. I had the privilege of seeing and reviewing (with white gloves) the original *Arizona Constitution of 1910* complete with its signatures and Seal. It is plainly typed, but it does display the golden pages of aging. Perhaps ironically, the earlier *Arizona Constitution of 1891* is a more beautiful work with its 79 pages of elegant calligraphy, though it does not carry the essential bearing of enactment.

The real beauty, of course, is in the form of government our Constitution proclaims. Perhaps not perfect, but it does preserve and protect Arizona by its principles of good government and provide the fundamental written acknowledgment of God.

Governor Hunt issued the call for the first state legislative assembly at the first possible date legal to do so: March 18, 1912. His first gubernatorial address to open the assembly began:

GOD IN THE FOUNDATIONS OF ARIZONA GOVERNMENT

"Grateful to Almighty God for the political liberty which has come to us; grateful for the spirit of American independence through which that liberty has been preserved to us; proud of the Arizona record which has preceded and led to this hour, and grateful for the privilege of participating in its momentous, never-to-be-forgotten events, I greet you, the chosen representative of the people of the sovereign State of Arizona..."
—p.226, History of Arizona, Vol. II, 1930

*Arizona's first state governor, George W. P. Hunt (1859-1934)
Photo by permission of Arizona State Library and Archives*

This concludes my brief review of our national and state historical foundations up to statehood. Certainly, there are many more details and other perspectives of our history remaining to be highlighted. I hope this provides a helpful beginning.

The Genesis of Government

*"So God created man in His own image; in the image of God He created him; male and female He created them. Then God blessed them; and God said to them, "Be fruitful and multiply; fill the earth and **subdue it**; have **dominion** over the fish of the sea, over the birds of the air, and over every living thing that moves on the earth."*
– Genesis 1:27-28

God created man in His own image, which includes the fundamental attribute to rule. This attribute was given at the very creation of man. It comes from the One Who created the universe and rules it. Kingship and government are essential attributes of God. When He made us in His image, He passed on to us a measure of His nature to govern.

The original Hebrew word in Genesis 1:28 is '*radah*' which means to take dominion, to rule, or to subjugate.

Obviously, we are all acutely aware of the abuses that are possible with governmental authority. Certainly God is aware of this, and thus the Bible provides extensive admonitions on how to rule justly, and historical testimony displaying the differing results of good kings and bad kings – good government and bad government – and their effect on people and nations.

In summation, the exercise of government is foundational to our nature. It comes directly and originally from God. The principles of good government are openly declared in the Bible. It is very counterproductive, then, when we attempt to take God and His word out of our government. He is the Author of government in the first place!

XII. Conclusion

> *"We pray, Lord, that the people shall not be disappointed; that they may have a constitution that will be a credit—that will stand on record for ages to come as a constitution perpetuating good government... Amen."*
>
> *– Chaplain Seaborn Crutchfield, November 10, 1910*

Foundations matter. Good foundations make a lasting difference. It has been my desire and humble privilege to look into the foundational history of our beloved Arizona. What I have discovered has convinced me that we have a solid governmental foundation in God as demonstrated by the written historical record.

This record begins with a Biblical basis in the history of nations, particularly focused, for our purposes, in the stream of English governmental charters leading to the dedication of America. Our national Founding Fathers then further incorporated Biblical principles in this great experiment called the United States of America into which Arizona was birthed.

In the Treaty of Guadalupe Hidalgo of 1848, The Gadsden Purchase of 1853, our original territorial actions of 1863, including the design of the Seal and Motto, in the practice of Oaths of Office, annual Thanksgiving Proclamations, and throughout our constitutional convention's pursuit of statehood—in all these we clearly see the mark of God.

The boldness, authority, and influence of men like Goodwin, McCormick, Hughes, Smith, and Crutchfield, and many others, all contributed to the written record affirming God in our foundation of good government.

However much it has been hidden, this foundation of God remains in our government. Like the foundation of most buildings, which give them their stability and strength, the foundations are generally below ground, buried, and often unnoticed, and even forgotten.

In my way of thinking, we can look at what is wrong and failed and human and sinful in our history, or we can look to what is good and right and just and properly honors God. The good things are the solid things that endure. By God's grace, we can build upon these.

From the place of God's grace we can then look at the other—the places where we have been wrong and fallen short of what is best—to ask for forgiveness and redemption, as we continue to declare our dependence on Him and work out our difficulties in humility together.

As I stated in my introduction, I am not saying that our founders were perfect or even exceptionally godly men. I am sure, should we have known them, we may have found them to be very much like us—full of weaknesses, faults, and failures. But I am deeply thankful for the good foundation that was laid down through them. I believe they honored God and we are thereby profoundly blessed.

When I first began this work, I had no idea that the history of God would be as deep and prevalent as I soon discovered. This is not a difficult history to unearth. However, the subject is so often maligned by many of our public institutions, or obscured by the continual inundation of new information in this age, that the incentive for re-discovery has been depressed.

I personally have been changed by this better understanding of our foundations. I hope that I have been able to communicate some of what I have discovered in such a way that brings more understanding and appreciation of God's hand in the affairs of our state and government.

The reader will notice that I have not even touched on the history of Christian churches in our nation or in Arizona. I have focused almost entirely on the written historical record within our government documents.

Nor do I believe I can be charged with presenting a partisan objective, for the historical figures mentioned have come from both sides of the political aisle. However, it is evident that the prevailing world view in our nation and in Arizona during our founding was Biblical, regardless of one's political affiliation. In that regard, I readily admit guilt in my partisanship for God.

> *"Then the Lord answered me and said, "Write the vision and make it plain on tablets, that he may run who reads it. For the vision is yet for an appointed time; but at the end it will speak, and it will not lie. Though it tarries, wait for it; because it will surely come, it will not tarry.""*
> *– Habakkuk 2:2-3*

There is something very important and historically significant about writing down vision. We have benefited greatly by this practice carried out with remarkable resolution by our Founding Fathers, both for America and Arizona. Let us be a generation, by the grace of God, who restore and build on this vision of the foundation of God in our government.

"Where there is no vision, the people perish."
– Proverbs 29:18, KJV

A few verses regarding prayer and the promises of God:

"If My people who are called by My name humble themselves, and pray and seek My face, and turn from their wicked ways, then I will hear from heaven, and will forgive their sin and heal their land. Now My eyes will be open and My ears attentive to prayer made in this place."
– 2 Chronicles 7:14-15

"Be anxious for nothing, but in everything by prayer and supplication, with thanksgiving, let your requests be made known to God." – Philippians 4:6

"Let us therefore come boldly to the throne of grace, that we may obtain mercy and find grace to help in time of need."
– Hebrews 4:16

"Therefore do not cast away your confidence, which has great reward. For you have need of endurance, so that after you have done the will of God, you may receive the promise." – Hebrews 10:35-36, 11:6

"For all the promises of God in Him are Yes, and in Him Amen, to the glory of God through us." – 2 Corinthians 1:20

"Thus says the Lord, 'Keep justice, and do righteousness, for My salvation is about to come, and My righteousness to be revealed. Blessed is the man who does this… Even them I will bring to My holy mountain, and make them joyful in My house of prayer… for My house shall be called a house of prayer for all nations.'" – Isaiah 56:1-2, 7

"The effective, fervent prayer of a righteous man avails much." – James 5:16

"Blessed is the nation whose God is the Lord, the people whom He has chosen as His own inheritance."
– Psalm 33:12

Appendix

i. Solemn Assembly for the State of Arizona – September 7, 2002

On Saturday, September 7, 2002 a Solemn Assembly was convened on the grounds of the State Capitol *"as a non-political, non-denominational gathering of Christians to acknowledge our desperate need for God in this critical time for our state and nation."* Approximately 1,000 representatives gathered from all over the state to participate in this 'Joel 2' event.

> *"Now, therefore," says the Lord, "Turn to Me with all your heart, with fasting, with weeping, and with mourning..." Consecrate a fast, call a sacred assembly; gather the people, sanctify the congregation... Let them say, 'Spare Your people, O Lord...' Then the Lord will be zealous for His land, and pity His people."* – Joel 2:12, 15-18

The timing of the Solemn Assembly was important for several reasons. First, the following Wednesday was the one-year anniversary of the tragedy of 9-11, and we were a nation in a declared war and under the threat of terrorist attack. The coming Tuesday was the critical Primary Elections of 2002. We were in the midst of a severe and extended drought, with the least recorded rainfall in decades. There were severe wildfires and bark beetle infestation that were decimating thousands of acres of Arizona forest, and even a mosquito pestilence "of Biblical proportions" (*Arizona Republic*, August 18, 2002)—see Joel, chapter 1.

Having never called a Solemn Assembly before, we had no idea what to expect, how many would show up, and what the response would be during and after the gathering. The leadership team for the event was formed by *Arizona Call to Prayer* (a ministry of *BridgeBuilders Int'l*) and *The Center for Arizona Policy,* along with a small council of pastors. In the weeks preceding the event we communicated various ways to prepare for the assembly by fasting and personal repentance. We also brought in Dr. Greg Frizzell to help lead the actual program. Dr. Frizzell had extensive experience in leading Solemn Assemblies.

We knew something significant was happening, when on the very day of the Solemn Assembly the heavens opened and it began to rain for the first time in several weeks. Ironically, we were concerned that this would dampen turnout. However, our concerns were proven wrong as people kept coming no matter how hard it rained. We were soaked, but during the three and half hours of the event from 5:30pm to 9:00pm, nobody left.

> *"The heavens also dropped rain at the presence of God...You, O God, sent a plentiful rain, whereby You confirmed Your inheritance, when it was weary."*   *– Psalm 68:8-9*

The format of the Solemn Assembly began with worship and opening prayers, then a specific sequence of personal "confessions and cleansing" of thoughts, attitudes, relationships, points of obedience to God's priorities, and for the Church of Arizona. We then made supplications for our cities, state, and nation. Finally, we concluded with prayers for revival and awakening, thanksgiving and praise to God. There was weeping. There was joy. There was the widespread sense that God was smiling upon us.

During the proceedings the rain at times would let up, even stop, and then in a remarkable way, pour down its hardest at precisely the time we prayed for rain for the state. The whole event was a moving encounter with God, and I believe a landmark for our state. We saw the immediate answers to prayer for rain and a beginning of the breaking of the drought, and then shocking, unexpected results in the Primary Elections. However, we knew that it was only the beginning of a process toward seeing righteousness restored.

ii. Recent Prayer Journey Accounts

I will attempt to summarize some of the dozens of intercessory prayer events I've had the privilege of coordinating in recent years. My purpose here is to encourage those who may not know that these types of activities are taking place in Arizona. A growing team of intercessors are intentionally, even methodically as God leads, covering many significant aspects of Arizona history and government in prayer. The focus of praying for good government is a relatively new development that is being exercised in many different ways.

Certainly, many, many more events and activities have occurred that I am unaware of that have significantly honored God. Even so, we know there is still much ground to cover.

SECURING OUR BORDERS

The event that began this more intentional approach of prayer journeys around Arizona was the response we had to the 9-11 tragedy. It was called "Securing our Borders", which *Arizona Call to Prayer* coordinated with our many county coordinators and other prayer-leader relationships. Within two weeks we were able to mobilize about 50 small teams of intercessors to pray simultaneously at 150 key locations throughout Arizona, such as at points along the border with Mexico and other states, at our power plants, dams, airports, government buildings, military bases, sports arenas, schools and large population centers.

This Saturday event not only served the purpose for which it was intended—to pray for God's protection at our "borders"—but had the added bonus of bringing together and connecting people of different churches and backgrounds. An experience such as this, with a clear mission and higher purpose, becomes an adventure that is shared which bonds together many of those participating. Each of these journeys is such an adventure. No two events are alike. They are unique, interesting, hard work and fun. They develop strong relationships, and provide a sense of accomplishment and transcendent purpose.

The other significant on-going prayer activities that contributed to an awareness of this approach of intentional on-site prayer were our annual participation in the National Day of Prayer and mountaintop prayer events.

MOUNTAINTOP PRAYER

"Come, let us go up to the mountain of the Lord!" – Micah 4:2

The Bible contains about 700 passages involving mountaintops, hilltops, high places, etc. *Moses receiving the Ten Commandments, Joshua, Elijah, Gideon, Ezekiel, the Sermon on the Mount, the transfiguration of Jesus...* mountaintops are places of vision, revelation, declaration, confrontation, authority, and encountering God.

Mostly in ignorance, but with a sense that "maybe there is something to this," I began mountaintop prayer in 1992 or 1993. Initially I hiked Camelback Mountain in central Phoenix to usher in the New Year at daybreak. Since then, a New Year's morning hike to the top of a mountain has been my tradition. Over the years, I have heard of many others that have been similarly inspired to mountaintop prayer.

> *"Let the wilderness and its cities lift up their voice...let them shout from the top of the mountains. Let them give glory to the Lord... The Lord shall go forth like a mighty man; He shall stir up His zeal like a man of war. He shall cry out, yes, shout aloud; He shall prevail against His enemies."*
> *— Isaiah 42:11-13*

On January 1, 2000, this became an annual, publicly promoted event through *Arizona Call to Prayer*. Small teams of intercessors have simultaneously hiked up several mountaintop locations throughout Arizona dedicating themselves, and the land before them, to God.

Mountaintop prayer is not confined to New Year's morning. There have been numerous prayer journeys to mountaintops at different times of the year for various specific purposes.

CORONADO NATIONAL MEMORIAL

For example, on May 10, 2003 we ascended to the panoramic view of Coronado National Memorial as part of a weekend prayer journey which had multiple stops in southern Arizona (Tucson–Benson—Tombstone—Bisbee—Naco—Coronado Memorial—Sierra Vista). At the Memorial we were able to pray over the border of Mexico laid out before us from horizon to horizon to the south, and over the whole San Pedro Valley, including Miracle Valley, and the route that the original conquistadors traveled under Coronado into the Southwest in 1540.

CROWN KING, ARIZONA

On Saturday, June 14, 2003 we met at the 'high place' of Crown King, a dirt street town of about 100 population which sits at an elevation of 5,911 feet near the geographic center of our state. Just two days before we were scheduled to go, a headline appeared in the *Arizona Republic* saying... *"Crown King in immense danger of fire."* It went on to state that Crown King was the *"Arizona community most in danger of a forest fire."* The timing was fascinating, since I had never heard of Crown King being mentioned before that headline. It is one of the original mining towns, "a living ghost town", in the Bradshaw Mountains established soon after Arizona became a territory. The area has a checkered history involving Native American conflicts, bloodshed, greed, and immorality. On that Saturday we gathered at *The Chapel of Crown King* and joined with Pastor Dan Woodward and others to worship, pray, and crown the King in the heart of Arizona.

MARS HILL AND HUMPHREYS PEAK – FLAGSTAFF

On Saturday, September 9, 2006, as part of 40 days of prayer and fasting called the *Siege in the Desert* leading up to the Primary Elections, there was a trip to Mars Hill (see Acts 17) in Flagstaff. Nine months later, on Saturday, June 9, 2007, intercessors from Northern, Central, and Southern Arizona joined together to climb to the top of the highest point of our state, Humphreys Peak, at 12,633 feet. In each place, prayers and banners to the Lord declaring "Lord of Hosts" and "Our God Reigns" were raised over the state. For an account of the Humphreys Peak event see www.arizonacalltoprayer.net.

EVENTS AT THE STATE CAPITOL

There have been dozens of prayer walks around the Capitol grounds, including annual prayer walks on the opening day of the legislative session in January, and as part of the National Day of Prayer on the first Thursday in May. Prayer walks are also a common practice as part of regular on-site prayer, especially during the legislative session from January through May each year. There was also a series of prayer walks on seven consecutive Monday mornings—a 'Jericho March'—leading up to the 2006 Primary Elections.

There have been numerous worship and prayer events at the State Capitol, especially in the last five years. Most of these have been called due to pending elections or key legislative issues. I already reviewed the first Solemn Assembly of 2002. There have been at least two more Solemn Assemblies since, and a large prayer rally was held on behalf of the protection of the Ten Commandments monument at Wesley Bolin Plaza on the Capitol grounds on September 27, 2003.

On May 17, 2005 a Marriage Crisis Rally was called on the day Massachusetts had determined to declare same-sex marriages legal. On that Monday, during a regular work day with school still in session, and 100+ degree weather, at Noon, an astounding 8,000 people showed up wearing white shirts at Wesley Bolin Plaza on the Capitol grounds. Though it wasn't a prayer event per se, it was about making a resolute stand for God's design for marriage. Choosing that time and place counter to all common sense was based on the leadership team's prayers to seek God's will. It was a phenomenal experience to see a sea of white, as families from every corner of Arizona came together as one. As far as we know, that was the single largest rally of that kind on the State Capitol grounds in history.

PRAYER AND FASTING

There has also been a wave of resurgence for the call and practice of fasting both individually and corporately in the last few years. Many individuals are taking up the practice of choosing a fast day each week as part of their regular spiritual discipline. Corporately there have been numerous specific calls for fast days, 7-day periods, and several 21-day and 40-day extended fasts called in conjunction with significant events on the political calendar. I strongly recommend a book by the late Derek Prince called *"Changing History through Prayer and Fasting"*.

2004 PRESIDENTIAL DEBATE

One of the most significant events that we have participated in with obvious national importance involved the Final Presidential Debate held on the campus of Arizona State University on Wednesday, October 13, 2004. At the time, the campaign between the Democratic nominee Senator John Kerry and Republican incumbent President George Bush was extremely heated. At stake was the direction the nation would take regarding the war and many key social and political issues. The candidates would determine very different paths for the future of our nation—it was time to pray.

In the weeks preceding the debate, we sent small teams to pray inside the host venue at Gammage Auditorium. We connected with local and statewide prayer ministries and developed an on-site prayer mobilization strategy for the event. Then, just a day or so before the debate, through the providence of God, the prayer participation would be multiplied into the millions!

An e-mail of prayer points and scriptures God had given us was picked up by the U.S. Strategic Prayer Network and sent to their 50 state coordinators, who sent them to thousands in each of their statewide networks. Another large national network, the Elijah List, forwarded the prayer points to their 116,000 intercessors. The Presidential Prayer Team sent the message to their two million-plus members. Suddenly, the nation was mobilized to pray the same thing at the same time.

Meanwhile, we organized 12 on-site prayer teams to be stationed at strategic locations around the host venue during the Presidential Debate. Each team had a specific prayer focus, including prayer for the candidates, safety and security issues, fairness of the moderator, and clarity on where each candidate stood on the vital issues.

On the day of the Presidential Debate, beginning at 4:00am, I suddenly began to receive a non-stop flood of calls on my cell phone by intercessors from all over the nation. My number had been included in the e-mail sent out to the Presidential Prayer Team! Though my cell phone was rendered useless to coordinate the on-site prayer on the ASU campus, it was well worth it to know first-hand the magnitude of the fervent and focused prayer occurring throughout, literally, every state of our nation for this pivotal event.

At ASU, the day began with mountaintop prayer on "A" Mountain overlooking the campus at daybreak. Various worship and prayer activities were held around the campus through the day, and throughout the Presidential Debate that evening from 6:00pm – 7:30pm. The whole campus was a circus with dozens of national media outlets broadcasting from tents, special agents and security everywhere, tens of thousands of university students and visitors, and all manner of strange attention-seekers.

The spiritual environment was highly charged as well. As we experienced the event and discussed the outcome, we knew that in the midst of it all, God was clearly active and exerted His authority. It is perhaps too soon to understand the full impact of such a time as that, but for those of us there, it was clear that God answered prayer.

40-DAY "SIEGE IN THE DESERT" I & II

Perhaps the most involved and strenuous corporate exercise of prayer and fasting to date were the commitments in 2006 by intercessors and worship teams to participate in two 40-day prayer and fasting *SIEGES*. "Siege I", from August 4 through September 12, led up through the Primary Elections. "Siege II", from October 1 through November 9, led up through the General Elections. Each "Siege" had a central location set up that provided a 24-hour-a-day headquarters for worship and prayer. Different teams took up assignments to cover nearly all these hours. All were committed to different types of fasts throughout the time period. It was a physically and spiritually demanding season, and filled with profound rewards and encounters with God.

It would be impossible to recount all the activity of these around-the-clock prayer times, (the journals themselves would fill a book) but they were focused on calling out to God for righteous leaders and good government in the elections, dealing with the sins of our society, and bringing about righteousness and justice in the land.

During these times, many prayer journeys were also conducted to such places as the site of the original Margaret Sanger *Planned Parenthood* family planning and abortion clinic and other similar locations in Tucson. On another Saturday, a prayer tour of all the major media outlets in Phoenix were covered by three intercessory teams.

There was also impacting national intercessory help during these two *SIEGES* through *The Call* youth aligned with Lou Engle. The value in building stronger relationships by going through this experience together was worth it all by itself.

THE NAVAJO SPRINGS ADVENTURE

Earlier, in the section of the book about the formation of the new Arizona Territory I spoke of a team traveling to Navajo Springs, Arizona on February 18, 2006, to the very place that the original territorial government party first officially organized. I will finish this section on 'prayer journeys' with a more detailed account of that trip:

Around 2004 I noticed a small plaque on the second floor of the State Capitol which mentions a list of Arizona government seats, including Navajo Springs as the place where Arizona's territorial government was first "organized." I wasn't sure what was meant by "organized" but I sat on the information without further research until January of 2006. Finally, my curiosity moved me to "google" 'Navajo Springs, Arizona' and brought me to a website that provided a map, descriptions, and reference books by Tom Jonas who had visited the location in 2000 and 2001. History books he referenced also revealed the enviable connection to President Abraham Lincoln and the circumstances surrounding the appointment of the governmental party that I have already discussed.

Jacob's Well, Arizona

At this point I must also mention a second historical target of our journey. The webpage on Navajo Springs included a small print link to another webpage referred to as "Jacob's Well." Intrigued by this Biblical name, I investigated.

The webpage included journal entries from western adventurers in the 1850s, such as describing a *"funnel-shaped depression, about 300 feet wide at the top, and 125 feet deep. Water is found at the bottom."* – May Humphreys Stacey, 1857.

> *"The water at the place of camping to-night is the greatest curiosity we have yet seen. In a wide level prairie, with no streams, there is an immense well about one hundred and fifty feet deep and six hundred in diameter. At the bottom is a large, deep pool of water – which it cost one a few minutes hard labor to reach." – David S. Stanley, 1853.*

I haven't discovered how *Jacob's Well* was given such a Biblical name, but I did discover that the Navajo name for the well is translated "Blessing of the Desert." This well is also mentioned in the journal by the governmental party just before they arrived at Navajo Springs in 1863.

What makes this more interesting is that this natural well, which had apparently been a primary watering place for the Navajos for centuries, rapidly became filled in by natural erosion (and due to increased use?) by the early 1900s. Today it is an unmarked 100-yard wide waterless depression in the desert with an old corral and a few trees nearby. Its existence is only verified by the website's research into the U.S. Geological Survey coordinates of old maps, and it is marked on a 1972 topography map put out by the USGS.

The Biblical name and the idea of spiritually "re-digging" *Jacob's Well* as a "Blessing of the Desert"—see Genesis 26 and John 4:6—and so closely aligned with the first organization of the Arizona Territory, further captured our imagination and intercessory juices for this trip.

Preparing for the Trip

I was now armed with information that could be dangerous. Intercessory friends agreed that it would be good to assemble a team that would travel to the actual site and pray. Within a few days we had a team, including pastors and experienced ministry leaders on "military alert" ready to make the four-hour trip from Phoenix at the first opportune time. Our wait primarily depended on receiving the proper permission to travel on Navajo Nation land.

We didn't have long to wait. The very next week during which Arizona's statehood day was celebrated (February 14), my co-coordinator for the trip, Anita Hensley, herself part Native American, received a phone call from a Navajo pastor who lives within 30 miles of Navajo Springs. She had been trying to reach him for a year. She also was able to get through to the Navajo authorities in the area.

Amazingly, the local ranger said he would leave us a packet containing a key to a locked gate, a hand-drawn map, and an official letter granting us permission to go on Navajo land. We had prayed for the Lord's favor and timing and it seemed clear the door was open to go. Immediately however, there was also a sense of spiritual warfare and, in fact, three team members had to bow out at the last minute due to sickness. That left us with 11 travelers.

The van set out at 5:30am on Saturday morning, February 18, 2006 from Phoenix going northeast through Payson to Heber to Holbrook then east to the I-40 "Navajo" exit. The travel time together provided for further preparations of prayer and reviewing the historical setting of the 1863 event. Upon arriving at the Travel Center at the Navajo exit, the packet provided by the ranger was waiting for us just as he had said.

We were also alerted that there was a monument in which we might be interested just east of the Travel Center alongside the access road onto the freeway. Sure enough, the small monument was a marker recording the Navajo Springs event of 1863, even including a portion of the first territorial governor's proclamation stating: *"to establish a government whereby the security of life and property will be maintained throughout its limits, and its varied resources be rapidly and successfully developed."* The monument did not give a date of its making, but it appeared relatively modern and it was the first we had heard of its existence. We knew by the photos we had that this was not the same monument as at the actual Navajo Springs site.

We then prayed at the roadside monument, including for such things as increasing good government for both Arizona and tribal governments, and for new resources to be unearthed for the Navajos. We read Isaiah 35 and prayed for healing and revival according to God's word for the desert. We had a time of repentance for the infamous 300-mile "Long Walk" forced upon the Navajos in 1864 by Kit Carson and his troops—the tragic and unjust uprooting of families with so many dying on the way to eastern New Mexico.

Our First Attempt at Finding Navajo Springs

Now we were ready to follow the ranger's hand-drawn map leading into reservation land. After proceeding a few miles south on the main road, we turned onto the designated unmarked dirt "road" amidst the rolling, high desert landscape essentially devoid of trees. The key the ranger provided opened a locked, swinging gate over a cattle guard.

We were to then pass over a second cattle guard and turn at the next trail to the right, proceeding until we arrived at Navajo Springs—sounded easy. However, after the second cattle guard nothing seemed to quite fit the description. Over the course of the next two hours we tried several trails without success.

At that point we decided to attempt the directions suggested on the Navajo Springs website by Tom Jonas. So, we went back to the main road, traveled some miles south to an eastbound road, then turned back to the north through a small village that was called "Navajo Springs." However, since we didn't have exact mileages to go by, as we passed about a dozen separated houses off to the left of the road (perhaps constituting "Navajo Springs"?) we thought we should go further in case something more in line with what we imagined the village to look like might appear over the next hill.

Finding Jacob's Well

After a few more "over the next hill" searches about five miles further down the road, we realized that the first cluster of houses was the only possible place that could be the village of Navajo Springs. However, we also realized we were probably now in the area of Jacob's Well described by the website. It should be just off to the right of this same road. The terrain and a small cluster of trees seemed to fit the description given, so we pulled to the side of the road and investigated.

Sure enough, we had happened onto the right spot. There, we asked God to open up wells of blessing in the desert. All we saw in the area was dry, sandy, cracked earth populated with desert shrubs. The unique situation of a river wash, large pieces of concrete, an old stick and wire corral, and the cluster of trees all confirmed the location. We prophetically "re-dug" the well a few inches with our bare hands. God will have to do the rest.

In the meantime, while waiting at the side of the road, we connected with the Navajo pastor from the area. We would now be a team of 12. Although the Navajo pastor had not previously heard of the historical significance of *Navajo Springs* or *Jacob's Well*, it was immediately apparent that he appreciated the significance of these locations. Further, it turns out he was a fourth generation direct descendent of one who had participated in the signing of significant treaties involving the Navajos during territorial days.

The Search for Navajo Springs

After some discussion, his counsel was to follow the original directions given by the ranger, since that was the way permission was actually granted. On Navajo land, one should abide by Navajo authority, so off we went back in pursuit of Navajo Springs via the cattle guard gate and dirt-rutted trails.

The pastor led in his pick-up. Soon we were seeing the same thing— that something wasn't right after the second cattle guard. We decided to drive a few miles further down the trail until we came upon another pickup, which was the first auto we had seen in hours. It was parked on a small hill overlooking some cattle at a watering hole.

The Navajo pastor went up to talk with them. After 20 minutes or so he returned with some possible guidance on where Navajo Springs might be. We piled back in our vehicles and retraced our route part way back, then turned to the south on a trail that looked like many others. There we saw a gated area surrounding what looked like another watering place. After more than four hours of searching, it was understandable that I heard someone mutter, *"Even if this isn't it, we'll consider it Navajo Springs!"*

After unleashing the metal wire ties to the gate we walked about 40 yards over to what looked like a monument or headstone. It was propped up in a dirt area sitting a few yards away from a steel-plate cylinder about 12 feet in diameter and four feet high. The headstone had fallen or been knocked off its base and now leaned against it. It said, *"St. John's in 1930"* – it looked like we were, once again, at a dead end. Then, we looked on the other side of the headstone, and there it was:

ARIZ. TERR.
GOVERNMENT
ORGANIZED HERE
DEC. 29, 1863

We had found it! Though somewhat deteriorated, it was the exact monument shown in the photos we had with us. We now knew, too, that the monument itself had been donated in 1930 somehow linked to "St. John's". Looking around, we saw marshy springs with reeds throughout the area, just as had been described in the 1863 account.

The cylindrical steel encasement, obviously added sometime in the 1900s, formed the walls of a deep well at the center of the springs. This was the place all right. We immediately experienced a strong sense of the historical significance of this simple but strategic place.

We gathered in a circle around the broken monument to pray with the marshy springs around about us on three sides. It was cold and very windy, piercing our layers of clothing. Sometimes the gusts would blow so that it was difficult even to hear each other in close proximity. From the history books we brought, we quoted the original proclamations issued by the newly sworn in Governor and Secretary of the Arizona Territory more than 140 years previously.

About the time we had knelt to pray and re-dedicate the land to God, we saw a pick-up truck advance down the dirt road toward us. A man came toward us, obviously angry, saying, *"how did you get here... you have no right to be on our land... you must leave right away..."* We were able to quietly say that we had received permission by the local ranger and had been given a key. We apologized that he had not been informed, and assured him of our good intentions.

Seeing no "fight" in us, and that we had been given authority to be there, he calmed down and explained that sometimes intruders would come shoot the antelope or cause other damage in the area, but local people like himself would get blamed. After a few more minutes he returned to his truck and was gone. This incident made it clear how important it had been for us to have gained the proper permission and to have the right key access. We knew it was spiritually significant to have the proper authority as well.

We then returned to pray and listen to our soft-spoken Navajo pastor-friend recount some history, open up some scripture, and give his sense of the significance of our time together. We huddled together closer in the cold and the wind, and he began to pray. He prayed a dedication and a blessing. At one point we discussed making a monument of stones in further dedication of the 'territory' to God.

After our Navajo friend quietly explained that the area was full of occult activity and that monuments of stones were set up at strategic places throughout the land, he suggested we make a monument of living stones instead. So, as we, the living stones, stood in a circle, we all leaned toward the middle and placed our right hands one upon the other and prayed. A pastor on our team then gave the Navajo pastor a gift of anointing oil from Israel. Following this, we knelt and prayed for healing of the land. We poured 'anointing' oil on the existing territorial monument "for good government" and then more on the ground "for healing of the land."

At this point, we weren't sure if we were within proper protocol. Our Navajo friend seemed to consider this for a moment, and then with a smile said, *"This is good, we have broken a stronghold here."*

Next, we acknowledged the fact that this original place of Arizona government is now on Navajo Nation land. We prayed for God to bring our governments together in a godly alignment, perhaps even into a partnership together. We prayed extensively for blessings upon the Navajo and all the tribes of Arizona. We prayed blessings upon our new Navajo friend and for an outpouring of revival among the Navajo—the largest tribe in the U.S.—and for the springs of salvation to come forth (Isaiah 12:3).

We noted that when we had finally arrived at Navajo Springs and assembled with the Navajo pastor leading us in prayer, it was 4:00pm, the same time in the afternoon that the Arizona Territorial government had organized at the same spot. It seems that even our wandering in the high desert looking for Navajo Springs had the timing of God on it, at least in this token way.

Given the relative inaccessibility and anonymity of Navajo Springs, we thought it very possible that this was the first time Christian prayer had been given at this place since December 29, 1863. And, if others have been led by God to this place in the past, we can only expect it has been at His direction building on His sure foundation. The 12 of us left this historic place of springs knowing that we did not arrive except by God's design and His grace. We also left having gained a new friend.

Upon returning to the Navajo Travel Center, we gave our Navajo pastor friend a spontaneous offering, and then began the drive home through the high desert full of thanksgiving while witnessing a magnificent Arizona sunset.

iii. Resources and References

The following is a list of resources and references that I have noted in this book and/or recommend for further study and support on this subject. Aside from this list is the vast resource of the Internet.

Arizona Democrat, Arizona Miner, Arizona Republic(an), Arizona (Globe) Silver Belt, Phoenix Gazette and other newspaper archives, kept at the *Phoenix Public Library*, Phoenix, Arizona, www.phxlib.org, and at the *Arizona State Library, Archives and Public Records*, and other historical archives listed below.

Arizona Historical Foundation, Hayden Library, Arizona State University, Tempe, Arizona, www.ahfweb.org.

Arizona Historical Society, locations in Flagstaff, Tempe, Tucson, and Yuma, Arizona, www.azhs.gov.

Arizona History Reference Guides, a website by Jeffrey Scott linking numerous resources at: http://jeff.scott.tripod.com/reference.html

Arizona Revised Statutes–Annotated, Volume 1, Constitutional Articles 1 to 5, Prepared under legislative authority, Laws 1956, Chapter 129, West Publishing Co., 1984.

(The) Arizona Room, 4th floor, Phoenix Public Library, 1221 N. Central Ave., Phoenix, Arizona 85004, www.phoenixpubliclibrary.org.

Arizona State Library, Archives and Public Records, History and Archives Division, State Capitol, Suite 342, 1700 West Washington, Phoenix, Arizona, 85007, website: www.lib.az.us

Adams, Ward R., *History of Arizona, Volume II,* Richard E. Sloan, Supervising Editor, Record Publishing Co., Phoenix, 1930.

Barton, David, Founder and President of *Wallbuilders* ministry, website: www.wallbuilders.com

Beliles, Mark A. and McDowell, Stephen K., *America's Providential History,* Providence Foundation, Charlottesville, Virginia, 1989.

Crippen, Alan R., II, *British Christianity and the American Order – Stephen Langton and the Magna Carta*, a paper, 2006, The John Jay Institute, Colorado Springs, CO 80903, www.johnjayinstitute.org

Farish, Thomas E., Arizona Historian, *History of Arizona*, Volume 3, Phoenix, Arizona, 1916, from the on-line *Books of the Southwest* collection of the University of Arizona Library.

Faulk, Odie B., *Arizona—A Short History*, University of Oklahoma Press, Norman, Oklahoma, 1970

Federer, William J., *America's God and Country- Encyclopedia of Quotations*, Amerisearch, Inc., St. Louis, Missouri, 1999.

Goff, John S., *Arizona Biographical Dictionary*, Black Mountain Press, Cave Creek, Arizona, 1983.

Goff, John S., *George W. P. Hunt and His Arizona*, Socio Technical Publications, Pasadena, California,1973.

Goff, John S., editor, *The Records of the Arizona Constitutional Convention of 1910*, The Supreme Court of Arizona, Phoenix, Arizona, 1991.

Gruver, Henry, *Crosswise – A Prayer Walker's Manual*, Joyful Sounds Ministries, P.O. Box 144, Woodbine, Iowa, 51579, 3rd Revision, 2003.

Henson, Pauline, *Founding a Wilderness Capital: Prescott, A. T. 1864*, Northland Press, Flagstaff, Arizona, 1965.

An Historical and Biographical Record of the Territory of Arizona, McFarland & Poole, Chicago, IL, 1896.

Jonas, Tom, websites for *Navajo Springs* and *Jacob's Well* in Arizona: www.tomjonas.com/swex/navajosprings.htm

Kelly, George H., Arizona Historian, *Legislative History Arizona 1864-1912*, Manufacturing Stationers, Phoenix, Arizona, 1926, includes the letter to Mr. Kelly: *"The Fight for Statehood"* from the Congressional perspective by former Arizona Senator Marcus A. Smith, pp. 287-302.

Keskel, Lt Col Kenneth, USAF, *The Oath of Office – A Historic Guide to Moral Leadership,* Air and Space Power Journal, Winter 2002.

Marshall, Peter J. Jr., and Manuel, David B. Jr., *The Light and the Glory*, Published by Fleming H. Revell, a division of Baker Book House Co., Grand Rapids, Michigan, 1977.

Martin, Douglas D., *An Arizona Chronology - The Territorial Years, 1846-1912,* University Press, Tucson, Arizona, 1963.

McClintock, James H., *Arizona, Volume 2*, S.J. Clarke Publishing Co., 1916.

Munsil, Len, *Arizona's Founding Fathers Had Firm Foundation*, Arizona Citizen magazine, published by *The Center for Arizona Policy*, September 1996.

Nicolson, John, editor, *The Arizona of Joseph Pratt Allyn, Letters from a Pioneer Judge: Observations and Travels 1863-1866*, The University of Arizona Press, Tucson, Arizona, 1974.

Perry, Richard L., editor, Cooper, John C., general supervisor, *Sources of Our Liberties- Documentary Origins of Individual Liberties in the United States Constitution and Bill of Rights*, Revised Edition, William S. Hein & Co., Inc., Buffalo, New York, 1991.

Prince, Derek, *Praying for the Government – How to Pray Effectively for the Nation and its Leaders*, a small booklet, Derek Prince Ministries International, 1992.

Prince, Derek, *Shaping History through Prayer and Fasting*, Whitaker House, New Kensington, Pennsylvania, 1973.

Sharlot Hall Museum and Archives, based at the restored territorial governor's house in Prescott, Arizona: www.sharlot.org/archives/

Sheets, Dutch, *Intercessory Prayer*, Regal Books, a division of Gospel Light, Ventura, California, 1996.

Winsor, Mulford, Arizona Historian, *The Arizona Constitution*, paper presented to teachers at the Arizona State Department of Library and Archives, January 30, 1946.

The 1864 Census of the Territory of Arizona, The Historical Records Survey, Phoenix, Arizona, 1938.

PHOTOGRAPHY and IMAGE CREDITS

PAGE   SUBJECT...

Cover ..... see image and photograph credits on p. 3.

Inside front cover... Arizona Territorial Seal of 1863, courtesy of the Arizona Secretary of State: www.azsos.gov/Info/state_seal/history

p. 27 .... *Moses and the Ten Commandments*, Rembrandt, public domain

p. 31 .... *Mayflower Compact* image, William Bradford journal, public domain

p. 33 .... First page of the *U.S. Constitution* image, public domain

p. 36 .... 1861 portrait of President Abraham Lincoln, public domain

p. 39 .... President George Washington, 1797, Gilbert Stuart, public domain

p. 43 .... Map of land acquisitions via *Treaty of Guadalupe Hidalgo* and *The Gadsden Purchase*, GNU Free Documentation license, courtesy Wikipedia, the free on-line encyclopedia

p. 45 .... Territorial Government Party Officials, 1863, courtesy of the Arizona Historical Foundation, origin unknown

p. 51 .... *Arizona Territory Proclamation,* 1863 (see cover description above)

p. 52 .... Navajo Springs monument photo by Rose Ann Tompkins, 2001, Tom Jonas website at: www.tomjonas.com/swex/navajosprings

p. 55 .... Governor John N. Goodwin, c.1864 (see cover description p.3)

p. 58 .... Arizona State Capitol, 1909, by permission of Arizona State Library, Archives and Public Records, #97-2558

p. 60 .... Senator Marcus Smith (see cover description p.3)

p. 66 .... Territorial Governor Louis Hughes, c.1890, by permission of Arizona State Library, Archives and Public Records, #99-9643

p. 68 .... *1894 Arizona Territorial Thanksgiving Day Proclamation*, courtesy of Arizona State Library, Archives and Public Records

p. 69 .... Constitutional Convention of 1910 members, with an inset of Seaborn Crutchfield, by permission of the Arizona State Library, Archives and Public Records, #95-2489

p. 79 .... Chaplain Seaborn Crutchfield, 1925 (see cover description p.3)

p. 145 ..... Secretary Richard McCormick, c.1860s (see cover description p.3)

p. 150-1... Arizona Seals of 1863 and current State Seal, courtesy of the Arizona Secretary of State: www.azsos.gov/Info/state_seal/history

p. 154 ..... Governor Geo. Hunt, 1912, by permission of Arizona State Library, Archives and Public Records, #97-6992

Photos of the author on page 14 in the 'Preface' sitting at the desk of the President of the Constitutional Convention of 1910 in the restored House chamber on the third floor of the original Capitol, and of the author in the desert on the back inside cover, courtesy of Garin M. A. Chadwick, 2007

Back cover Arizona State Seal (see above description from p. 150-1)

THE TWO FOUNDATIONS

"Therefore whoever hears these sayings of Mine, and does them, I will liken him to a wise man who built his house on the rock: and the rain descended, the floods came, and the winds blew, and beat on that house; and it did not fall, for it was founded on the rock.

"But everyone who hears these sayings of Mine, and does not do them, will be like a foolish man who built his house on the sand: and the rain descended, the floods came, and the winds blew and beat on that house; and it fell. And great was its fall."

— Jesus speaking, Matthew 7:24-27

THE BUILDER AND MAKER IS GOD

"By faith Abraham obeyed when he was called to go out to a place which he would receive as an inheritance. And he went out, not knowing where he was going... for he waited for a city which has foundations, whose builder and maker is God."

— Hebrews 11:8, 10

BUILDING THE FOUNDATIONS

*"Oh Lord and Gracious Heavenly Father, we again thank Thee for our past blessings, of health, peace and happiness, and the privilege of meeting again in convention assembled, and we ask that Thou wouldst continue Thy mercies and blessings upon our heads through this day. Take us by the hand and lead us safely through the labors and tasks of another day, for we would not undertake this work without Thine aid and assistance. In all the labors that are before us, we would that wisdom should be our guide and that our acts may be accounted unto us for good and for the good of this country and this great State which these men are now **building the foundations**. Lead us ever in the straight and narrow way and when we have finished our building and our work here on earth save us we pray Thee in Thy Kingdom above, is our supplication in the Name of Thy Son Jesus Christ, our Savior, Amen."*

— Chaplain Seaborn Crutchfield
Wednesday morning, October 26, 1910, p. 85,
The Records of the Arizona Constitutional Convention of 1910

About the author...

Guy Chadwick was born in Richmond, Virginia in 1957. While growing up, his family moved frequently due to his father's job promotions, and he lived in eight cities in six states before first arriving in Arizona in 1973.

He graduated from Scottsdale Chaparral High School, and then Arizona State University—*Summa Cum Laude*. At ASU, he also began a competitive national and international badminton career as a player and a coach that continues to the present.

In 1985, he was blessed to marry his wife, Teri, and they have three children—Kia, Dane, and Garin—whom they have homeschooled, the first two having graduated thus far.

Guy has served as a deacon, elder, or on a pastoral staff in the non-denominational Christian churches where he and his family have been members since the mid-1990s. In the late 1990s he became more specifically involved as a coordinator of various Christian events. This developed into the overlapping coordinator roles with *The Center for Arizona Policy*, April 2002 through January 2007, and with *Arizona Call to Prayer*, from 2000 to the present, which he now co-directs with Cheryl Sacks.

He has a love of the people, the land, and the history of Arizona that flows into hiking (especially with his wife), research, and worship and prayer journeys throughout the state. Mountaintop prayer is one of his favorite activities. Seeing an Arizona 'house of prayer' established is one of his great desires. Forging deep friendships along the way makes it all worth while.

Guy is still amazed that God has placed him in this rather unique and sometimes challenging position as a governmental prayer coordinator—***and he loves it!***